THE GREAT LIVES SERIES

Great Lives biographies shed an exciting new light on the many dynamic men and women whose actions, visions, and dedication to an ideal have influenced the course of history. Their ambitions, dreams, successes and failures, the controversies they faced, and the obstacles they overcame are the true stories behind these distinguished world leaders, explorers, and great Americans.

**Other biographies in the Great Lives Series**

*CLARA BARTON: Founder of the American Red Cross*
*CHRISTOPHER COLUMBUS: The Intrepid Mariner*
*AMELIA EARHART: Challenging the Skies*
*THOMAS EDISON: Inventing the Future*
*JOHN GLENN: Space Pioneer*
*MIKHAIL GORBACHEV: The Soviet Innovator*
*JESSE JACKSON: A Voice for Change*
*JOHN F. KENNEDY: Courage in Crisis*
*MARTIN LUTHER KING: Dreams for a Nation*
*ABRAHAM LINCOLN: The Freedom President*
*GOLDA MEIR: A Leader in Peace and War*
*SALLY RIDE: Shooting for the Stars*
*FRANKLIN D. ROOSEVELT: The People's President*
*HARRIET TUBMAN: Call to Freedom*

A special thanks to educators Dr. Frank Moretti, Ph.D., Associate Headmaster of the Dalton School in New York City; Dr. Paul Mattingly, Ph.D., Professor of History at New York University; and Barbara Smith, M.S., Assistant Superintendent of the Los Angeles Unified School District, for their contributions to the Great Lives Series.

# GREAT LIVES

# NELSON MANDELA
## *A VOICE SET FREE*

By Rebecca Stefoff

FAWCETT COLUMBINE
NEW YORK

For middle-school readers

A Fawcett Columbine Book
Published by Ballantine Books

Copyright © 1990 by The Jeffrey Weiss Group

All rights reserved under International and Pan-American Copyright Conventions. Published in the United States by Ballantine Books, a division of Random House, Inc., New York, and simultaneously in Canada by Random House of Canada Limited, Toronto.

Library of Congress Catalog Card Number: 90-93126
ISBN: 0-449-90570-5

Cover design and illustration by Paul Davis Studio

Manufactured in the United States of America

First Edition: September 1990

10 9 8 7 6 5 4

# TABLE OF CONTENTS

**Chapter 1**
   "At the Island"                                    1
**Chapter 2**
   An African Heritage                                9
**Chapter 3**
   A Land of Beauty and Strife                       23
**Chapter 4**
   Journey to Johannesburg                           33
**Chapter 5**
   Family Man, Young Politician                      42
**Chapter 6**
   Apartheid and Resistance                          58
**Chapter 7**
   Sharpeville and the Underground                   71
**Chapter 8**
   Two Trials                                        84
**Chapter 9**
   The World's Most Famous Prisoner                  96
**Chapter 10**
   Winds of Change                                  108
**Chapter 11**
   *The Struggle Is My Life*                        122

**Pronunciation Key**                               132

# 1

## "At the Island"

MAY 24, 1963, DAWNED clear and bright over Pretoria, one of the three capital cities of the Republic of South Africa. The rays of the rising sun glinted on the rooftops and windows of the massive government buildings on Meintjes' Kop, a hill that overlooks the city. South of the city they sparkled on the Voortrekker Monument, a 120-foot-tall granite tower that honors the *voortrekkers*, pioneers of Dutch descent who were the ancestors of many of South Africa's present-day white citizens.

The sun also shone down on Pretoria Central Prison. For the prison's inmates, however, the day was to be anything but bright. Four of them were political prisoners, serving time for crimes against the state—crimes of conscience, as the prisoners called them. All were black Africans. They had grown up in a country that would not let them vote because they were black, a country that deprived them of many rights enjoyed by white South Africans. Each had taken up the struggle against this racial oppression.

One of them was Nelson Mandela, a 44-year-old hero of South Africa's beleaguered equal rights movement. He had been arrested months earlier after eluding a nationwide manhunt for more than a year. He was now serving a five-year sentence for two crimes: encouraging black workers to go on strike and leaving the country without a passport. He had expected to serve out his sentence in the Pretoria prison, which was not too far from his home in the nearby city of Johannesburg. On this day, however, he learned otherwise.

Without preparation or warning, he was told that he was being transferred to another prison. He was not told where. Within an hour, he and three others were pushed inside a closed van and were rolling through the prison gates.

Mandela's companions were John Gaitsiwe, Steven Tefu, and Malete. Gaitsiwe was an organizer of trade unions for black workers. Tefu was an older man who was admired by many of the prisoners at Pretoria for his fighting spirit. He regularly complained of the harsh prison conditions and refused to knuckle under to the warders. Malete had been a reporter for *New Age*, the newspaper of the Congress Movement, which was a loose association of groups that opposed the white government. Mandela was one of the leaders of a powerful organization within the Congress Movement called the African National Congress, or ANC.

Inside the van, the four men were shackled together with chains. Each of them was also handcuffed. They sat on a platform along one side of the compartment, trying not to jostle one another or pull against their shackles whenever the van crossed a rough stretch of road. When night fell, they were grateful for the warmth of each other's bodies in the unheated van. They were provided with a bucket to use as a toilet; the stench from the bucket inside the closed van became almost unbearable. The prisoners talked and sang, and when they could they snatched a few precious moments or hours of sleep.

The van finally came to a stop around noon the following day, and the shackles were unfastened. The four men stepped out into a small courtyard, blinking at the light after so many hours in the gloomy interior. They soon learned that they were at the Roeland Street jail in Cape Town, another of South Africa's capital cities. At that moment, any lingering doubts that the prisoners might have had about their ultimate destination disappeared. Now they knew where they were bound.

Cape Town, the site of the first white settlement in South Africa, is located at the southwestern tip of the African continent. The city is bounded on the east by the rugged slopes of a majestic, flat-topped bluff called Table Mountain. On the west, it faces the chilly southern Atlantic Ocean. Cape Town has a broad, curving harbor known as Table Bay, famous for both its scenic beauty and its good anchorages. And in the center of Table Bay is a speck of limestone rock called Robben Island.

The island has served several purposes in South Africa's history. At one time it was a leper colony, where victims of the incurable illness that is now called Hansen's disease were confined. During World War II it was a naval station, part of the Allied defense against German submarines in the

South Atlantic. But during South Africa's long history of racial conflict, Robben Island has been best known as a prison. As early as 1658, only half a dozen years after the Dutch founded their first permanent settlement, an African chieftain was imprisoned on Robben Island after a series of battles between the whites and the native Khoikhoi people of the area. The chief's tribal name was Autshumayo, although the white historians called him Harry the Strandloper, which means "beachcomber" in Afrikaans, the Dutch-based language of the settlers. Autshumayo managed to escape from the island. He is the only prisoner who has ever done so.

During the next two centuries, as the white settlers increased in number and spread north and east from Cape Town, conflicts between the whites and various African tribal groups grew more frequent and bitter. The Xhosa were noted for their particularly determined resistance against the whites. Two Xhosa military commanders, Makana and Maqoma, were captured and imprisoned on Robben Island in the 1800s. Langalibalele, a chief of the Hlubi people, was sentenced to life imprisonment on the island in 1873. His resistance to white rule was regarded as treason by the British, who controlled part of South Africa at that time. By 1963, Robben Island was no longer a naval fortress, as it had been during World War II. It had been restored to its earlier use and was once again a prison.

No one loves a prison, but Robben Island is especially feared and hated by black Africans, who call it *esiqithini*, which means "at the island." To many Africans, when someone is *esiqithini*, it means he is also a hero of the resistance against white rule. At the time of Mandela's arrival, the white government hoped that the prisoners on the island, out of sight and out of touch with their followers, would be forgotten by the world. But South Africa's blacks had not forgotten the earlier heroes and freedom fighters who had been sent there. They would not forget Nelson Mandela, either.

Mandela and his three companions remained at the Roeland Street jail until evening fell. Then they were taken to an old district of docks and warehouses and ordered to board a waiting prison boat, where they were confined to the hold belowdecks. The boatmen cast off the lines and the boat pulled away from the dock. Mandela knew that a grim new chapter in his life was about to begin.

When the boat docked, the prisoners were herded onto the wharf and met by a group of prison warders, or guards, armed with rifles. One of them greeted the new arrivals with the ominous announcement, "This is not Pretoria. This is Robben Island."

All four men knew that the warders wanted to terrify and intimidate them. They also knew that the entire course of their lives on the island would depend upon how they handled this first confrontation with the prison authorities. If they gave in now to fear and intimidation, they would find it hard to recover any independence or dignity later.

"Huck! Huck! Huck!" cried the guards. This is the cry that farm boys in South Africa use when herding cattle. The prisoners were expected to fall obediently into place and to move along in a shuffling trot at the warders' command. It was a crucial moment.

Calmly, but without hesitation, Mandela and Steven Tefu, the defiant elder, stepped to the front of their little group and began walking forward at a measured, dignified pace. The others followed. The warders angrily called out "Huck! Huck!" louder this time, trying to force the men to walk faster. The prisoners did not break stride.

All at once the guards began shouting, "Do you want us to kill you? We will kill you!" They poked at the prisoners with the barrels of their rifles. Despite the threats and harassment, the prisoners walked steadily at their own pace all the way to the prison gates. They passed beneath a guardpost manned with warders whose guns were firmly pointed at the prisoners. Mandela knew that if he tried to run or struck back at one of the guards who was jabbing at him with a rifle, he would be shot on the spot.

Inside the prison, a room had been prepared for the reception of new prisoners. Orderlies had washed down the floor with buckets of water. In the middle was a big puddle into which the prisoners were made to stand. A guard shouted, "Strip!" and the men took off their clothes. The garments were snatched from their hands and dropped into the water. After a thorough physical search by an orderly from the prison hospital, the prisoners were left standing naked in the puddle on the cold stone floor.

An officer named Captain Gericke inspected them. Gericke noticed that Mandela and Malete had managed to avoid having their heads shaved at the Pretoria prison. "Why is your hair so long?" he demanded of Malete. Then he turned to Mandela and added, insultingly, "Like this boy's." Gericke went on to make it clear that the prisoners could expect no such soft treatment at the Island.

"Look here—" Mandela began when Gericke paused for breath.

At once Gericke turned upon him in anger, waving a finger under Mandela's nose and telling him to be quiet.

Mandela coolly replied, "I must warn you I'll take you to the highest authority, and you'll be as poor as a dormouse by the time I finish with you."

The captain was thunderstruck by what must have seemed to him to be outrageous insolence from a black prisoner. He leveled a string of curses at Mandela and then shouted, "You are going to do five years, and you show such cheek!"

"Don't be laughable," Mandela replied calmly. "I will not allow you to do anything outside the regulations."

Gericke was so surprised—and so infuriated—that he sputtered with rage, becoming speechless.

Another officer, Colonel Steyn, tried to weaken the spirits of the prisoners by turning them against one another. He said to Mandela, who had earned a law degree and practiced law in Johannesburg, "You and I, Mandela, are educated men. *We* have common interests." Then he turned to Tefu, "Unlike you. You are rotten!"

The older man proudly straightened his skinny shoulders and contemptuously declared to the colonel, "I am Steven Tefu, and I am known all over the world. More people know me than know your prime minister!"

The inspection was over. The prisoners dressed and were marched to their cells. Mandela's was a small, solitary cubicle of gray stone. It was lit by one 40-watt light bulb. Its furnishings consisted of a bedroll and a bucket. He had no sooner taken in the bleakness of his new surroundings than the door shut behind him with a hollow clang.

For all Mandela knew, he would be spending the remaining four and a half years of his sentence in this room. As it turned out, he was to occupy many prison cells over the coming months and years. But one thing he could not have foreseen on that May evening in 1963 was that nearly three decades would pass before he was free again. Nor could he have known that while those decades slowly passed, he would become the world's most famous prisoner and that he would one day be recognized and honored around the world as a symbol of the struggle for freedom and racial equality in South Africa.

# 2

## An African Heritage

ON JULY 18, 1918, a baby boy was born to a man named Hendry Mphakanyiswa Gadla Mandela at a place called Mbhashe, near the city of Umtata in southeastern South Africa. Mbhashe was located in a region that was once called Thembuland, after the Thembu people that inhabited it. Today, Thembuland is part of the black state within South Africa that is called the Transkei.

In 1918, Thembuland was a quiet and remote backwater, a land of sun-scorched grasslands, rolling hills, and wide expanses of blue sky. Much of the Transkei today looks just as it did then. Many of its present inhabitants live the same way Hendry Gadla lived, in small villages where each house has a *kraal*, or cattle pen, containing a few cattle and goats as well as a garden of corn and vegetables scratched out of the dry earth.

The mother of Hendry Gadla's new son was Nosekeni Fanny Mandela. Although the boy was her first child, he was not the first child for her hus-

9

band. Hendry Gadla Mandela, who was descended from a king of the Thembu people, was a minor chief and fairly prosperous by local standards. He owned a riding horse, for one thing and, at a time when wealth was measured in cattle, he owned a sufficient number to be able to afford more than one wife. He therefore, as was the custom among his people, had four wives at the same time. Some of them had already borne children. Nosekeni Fanny was his third wife.

Hendry Gadla's new son was baptized in the local Methodist church. Although Hendry Gadla was not a Christian, Nosekeni Fanny was. At his baptism, the baby was given the name Rolihlahla Nelson Dalibhunga Mandela. Like the names of his father, his mother, and many of his relatives, his was a mixture of traditional African names— particularly those that were favored by the Thembu tribe—and English-language names acquired from the British. The boy was often called Nelson. He also had a nickname, Buti. The three daughters later born to Hendry Gadla and Nosekeni Fanny usually used this nickname to refer to their big brother.

Not long after Nelson was born, Hendry Gadla Mandela moved his growing family to a settlement called Qunu, still in the Umtata district. Here each of his wives built her own home, according to Thembu custom. Nosekeni Fanny's home consisted of three small huts called rondavels. These were probably round in shape and made of mud brick, as this was the most common type of rondavel at that time.

The men in the family helped Nosekeni Fanny by adding the rondavels' roofs, which were made

Shortly after Nelson Mandela was born in 1918, his family moved to this settlement called Qunu, in the Transkei. Nelson's father had four wives, each with her own farm, according to the custom of the Thembu tribe. The round buildings are called rondavels. One was used as a kitchen, another for storage, and a third for sleeping. This is what Nelson's mother's farm looks like today.

of thatched leaves and straw. One of the rondavels was used for cooking. It had a stove that consisted of a hole in the ground with a metal grate laid over it. There was no chimney to carry the smoke away, only a small window, so the kitchen rondavel was always warm and smoky when meals were being prepared. A second rondavel was used for storing corn and other food supplies. The third and largest was for sleeping. It was furnished in the simple traditional African style, with stools for sitting and mats on the ground for sleeping. There were no pillows. Nelson slept curled on his side, with an elbow under his head for support.

Like all married women, Nosekeni Fanny also had her own kraal and cornfield. She planted the corn (called mealies throughout South Africa), tended it, and harvested it. She stripped the kernels from the cobs, ground them into flour between two stones, saved the cornmeal in clay pots and straw baskets in the storage rondavel, and baked the meal into bread. The girls learned these tasks at her side while they were still babies.

As soon as Nelson was old enough to walk and carry a stick, he took on the traditional chore of small boys throughout Africa—tending the family livestock. He led the cows and goats out of the kraal in the morning and back into it at night. The herd provided a sufficient supply of milk, but the field did not yield enough corn to feed the family, so Nosekeni Fanny had to buy extra. Nonetheless, her children never felt poor. They grew up feeling that their way of life was fairly comfortable.

One aspect of life that the children simply took for granted was the extended, interconnected nature of African families. Each of Hendry Gadla

Mandela's wives had her own household, but the households were close together. The four wives had a total of twelve children, and for the most part the children worked and played together happily and harmoniously. Nelson's sister Nomabandla, who was called Leabie, recalls, "Our kraal at Qunu was very busy and I had plenty of older sisters to advise me and sisters my own age to play with."

When he grew older and began to study tribal history, Nelson learned that rivalries between sons of the same man by different mothers had sometimes led to conflict and even warfare among the Thembu and other African peoples. All the same, he appreciated the duties and advantages of kinship. The responsibilities were simple and were known to all. Every African boy or girl was expected to be able to give an accurate and detailed account of his or her own ancestry and that of dozens of brothers, sisters, cousins, aunts, and uncles. A relative was never turned away from one's door. Instead, you offered shelter, food, and hospitality to any relative who needed it, however distant the relationship.

The advantages of kinship were many, but the most important was that no one was ever left completely alone, without resources or support. Throughout his life, Nelson Mandela has been grateful for the help and comfort he has received from the wide-ranging members of the Madiba clan to which he belongs by birth. Madiba was a Thembu ancestor about eight generations before Nelson.

"Our families are much larger than those of whites," he once wrote to a cousin. "And it's always pure pleasure to be fully accepted through-out a village, district, or even several districts occupied by your clan as a beloved household member, where you can call at any time, completely relax, sleep at ease and freely take part in the discussion of all problems, where you can even be given livestock and land to build free of charge."

He went on to say, "I have a lot of respect for this institution, not only because it's part of me, but also due to its usefulness. It caters for all those who are descended from one ancestor and holds them together as one family." But he recognized that sweeping changes in African society have affected the ancient institution of the extended family. He wrote, "It's an institution that arose and developed in the countryside and functions only in that area. The flocking of people to the cities, mines, and farms makes it difficult for the institution to function as in the old days."

Nelson's childhood was spent deep in the countryside, however, and rural traditions were still strong and unchanged. So it was natural for his father to consult the head of the clan when the time came to make plans for the boy's future.

Nosekeni Fanny became worried about her son's future. She knew that the minor chieftainship held by Hendry Gadla would one day pass, not to Nelson, but to Hendry Gadla's brother in another branch of the clan. So Hendry Gadla decided that his son ought to have an education in order to secure a good job. The Qunu school offered only the first few grades. Hendry Gadla spoke with his nephew Jongintaba David Dalindyebo, who was the senior chief of all the Thembus and the head of the Madiba clan. Chief Jongintaba agreed to make himself responsible for Nelson's education. This was in keeping with tribal tradition.

For the first nine years of his life, Nelson lived at Qunu with his family, playing and doing chores and working his way through the lower grades of the local school. But in 1927, Hendry Gadla Mandela died. He had suffered financial setbacks and left his family with little of his former wealth. But Chief Jongintaba was mindful of his responsibility to his young kinsman and sent word that the boy was to come live with him at his home in Mqekezweni. Fifty years later, Nelson recalled those troubled days.

"Mother could neither read nor write and had no means to send me to school. Yet a member of our clan educated me from the elementary school right up to Fort Hare [that is, college] and never expected any refund. According to our custom, I was his child and his responsibility."

Nelson was to spend the rest of his boyhood in Jongintaba's household at Mqekezweni. Eventually the other members of his family moved away from Qunu, and today there are no Mandelas living there. But the graves of Nelson's ancestors can still be seen on a Qunu hillside.

Like Qunu, Mqekezweni is in Thembuland, in the Umtata district. It was the seat of power for the Thembu kings in bygone times. Jongintaba's father Dalindyebo was chief there before him, and Ngangelizwe before him, and Mtirara before him. Mtirara's father was King Ngubengcuka, who was also the father of Hendry Gadla's grandmother. Both Nelson Mandela and Chief Jongintaba were thus descended from Ngubengcuka. And Ngubengcuka's great-great-grandfather was Madiba, from whom the entire clan is descended.

Nelson Mandela has given the world no record of his feelings on that long-ago day when he arrived at his new home, having left his mother and sisters in Qunu, where his father was newly buried. But a cousin named Ntombizodwa, who was four years older than Nelson, saw him on his first day in Mqekezweni.

"I remember clearly the day he came," she says. "He was in khaki shorts and a khaki shirt. He was shy and, I think, lonely. So at first he didn't say much."

Nelson's possessions—mostly simple clothes—were stored in a tin trunk. He and his trunk were moved into a small rondavel that he shared with one of Jongintaba's sons, a boy named Justice. "The two boys were as brothers," recalls Ntombizodwa. She adds that Nelson quickly formed a warm and supportive relationship with Nkosikasi No-England, who was one of Jongintaba's wives. "I think she loved him as much as she did her own boy, Justice, and Nelson returned that love and came to see her as if she was his own mother."

Mqekezweni was and still is a farming community, like Qunu. It lies in hilly country, cut with ravines and baked by the sun. Here and there are clusters of rondavels with roofs of thatch or corrugated metal. Their sides are painted white or green. Sheep, goats, and cows stray across the rutted roads, for the traffic is slight and there are few fences. The most important buildings in the community today are the same ones that shaped Nelson's boyhood: the square school with the patched iron roof where he finished his elementary education; the church he attended on Sundays; the simple redbrick courthouse across the road from the church; and the royal dining hall, three rondavels connected under one thatched roof, where Chief Jongintaba shared meals and conversation with visitors. During these state meals, Nelson and the other boys waited on the men. The youngsters kept silent but listened eagerly to everything that was discussed. They were enthralled by the news and stories their elders shared over food and drink.

Mandela's cousin remembers that Nelson was diligent in his attendance at both school and church. He also carried out his chores faithfully. The boys and girls attended school together. English, geography, history, and Xhosa (one of the principal African languages of South Africa) were the first subjects Nelson studied. After school each day, he would change out of his good khaki shorts and shirt and into older, more worn clothes. He and the other boys would then set out for several hours of what the girls called "romping in the fields," which was really cattle herding.

Every evening the boys would milk the cows and carry the pails of milk to Jongintaba's head wife. There was no electricity in Mqekezweni, so any studying that needed to be done in the evening was done by oil lamps. Most of the time, however, everyone went to sleep soon after nightfall, because the day started early. As soon as the edge of the sun cleared the horizon, it was time to take the cows out to pasture.

School, church, and chores did not take up all of Nelson's time. There were also games and sports with his cousins. They hunted birds with slingshots, roasted their catch on sticks over an open fire, and feasted. Their favorite pastime was racing Jongintaba's horses. This was a rare treat, for horses were quite valuable and the chief did not often let the boys ride them.

In 1985, Nelson Mandela described his boyhood in Mqekezweni in a letter to a friend. He wrote: "I have the most pleasant recollections and dreams about the Transkei of my childhood, where I hunted, played sticks, stole mealies on the cob, and where I learned to court; it is a world which is gone. A well-known English poet had such a world in mind when he exclaimed: 'The things which I have seen I now can see no more.' " Mandela may have been especially nostalgic for his carefree childhood when he wrote this letter because it was written after he had spent more than twenty years in prison.

One other part of Nelson's boyhood deserves attention. More than church or school or family, it helped to mold his thinking and direct the course of his life. This was the education in African lore that he received as he listened to the talk of the tribal elders who paid visits to Jongintaba. His cousin Ntombizodwa recalls, "The chiefs and headmen from all the districts came to Mqekezweni and, their business done, they would sit in the dining hall and talk. As children we listened and we heard a history that was not written in our history books."

Nelson's favorite among the chiefs was a very old man named Zwelibhangile Joyi. The children called him Tatu Joyi. *Tatu* is a term of respect and affection that means something like "grandfather." Tatu Joyi was skinny and shriveled and hunched. His skin was so dark that he looked blue, and he was extremely wrinkled with age. His frail body was racked with convulsions of coughing. Yet this old man had been a soldier in the army of the Thembu chief Ngangelizwe, Jongintaba's grandfather, who had fought to preserve the independence of his people from the conquering British. As old as Tatu Joyi was, Ntombizodwa remembers that when he told stories about the olden days and the bygone glories of the Thembu chiefs "the years dropped from his body and he danced like a young warrior."

From Tatu Joyi, Nelson learned how the various tribal groups were related. The Zulu, the Thembu, the Pongo, the Xhosa, and others were all *abantu*. Each group was different, yet each was part of a southern African whole that had once been proud and united. Chiefs in the old days governed each *isizwe* ("nation") with respect and love for their subjects—or else they were overthrown. Land belonged not to individuals but to the isizwe, and was used for the good of all. And always, in Tatu Joyi's telling, it was the coming of the whites that brought greed, violence, and evil into the African paradise. The whites tricked the Africans into signing away their lands. They set brother against brother, Tatu Joyi said, encouraging the sons of the chiefs to fight with one another. When such fights had weakened the tribes, the white men came in force with their foreign weapons and seized the land.

One tale told by Tatu Joyi concerned the Xhosa people, who had fought spiritedly for more than a century against the oncoming whites. Fearing that they would be unable to defeat the Xhosa on the battlefield, the whites finally planned a terrible trick. They cunningly faked voices that claimed to be the *izinyanya*, the ancestral spirits that were deeply revered in all the pre-Christian religions of Africa. A false izinyanya tricked a wise man of the Xhosa into believing that "Russians" would come to help the Xhosa defeat the British. Pretending to be the wise man's dead brother, the false izinyanya—who was really an Englishman in some sort of disguise—said that if the Xhosa killed their cattle and destroyed their cornfields, the Russians would come and the Xhosa would be victorious over the British.

The Xhosa chiefs were afraid to offend the izinyanya, so they did as the false spirits had told them to do. But the result was not a glorious victory: it was famine, disease, and finally defeat. The British gained control of Xhosaland, then Thembuland in 1885, and finally Pondoland.

Recalling the many childhood evenings that were spent listening to Tatu Joyi spin his stories of courage and betrayal while the leaping firelight played on his fierce old face, Ntombizodwa says, "We were all thrilled by his tales, but especially Nelson. I could see it did something to him, so that I am sure that Tatu Joyi's tales lived with him always." She adds, "We listened to Tatu Joyi and it made us angry that the British had done these things to us and ashamed that our ancestors had allowed these things to happen to them. Even then I saw that Nelson's anger was the greatest of all. That is why he has spent his life in prison. He told the court of these things when they sentenced him.

I could not be there, but I read every word he said and it was true and I heard Tatu Joyi in those words."

The words Ntombizodwa speaks of were those spoken by Nelson Mandela at his trial in 1962. He began a long and eloquent address to the court this way: "Many years ago, when I was a boy brought up in my village in the Transkei, I listened to the elders of the tribe telling stories about the good old days, before the arrival of the white man. Then, our people lived peacefully under the democratic rule of the kings and moved freely and confidently up and down the country without let or hindrance. Then the country was our own. We occupied the land, the forests, the rivers; we extracted the mineral wealth beneath the soil and all the riches of this beautiful land. We set up and operated our own government, we controlled our own armies and we organized our own trade and commerce. The elders would tell tales of the wars fought by our ancestors in defence of the fatherland, as well as the acts of valor by our generals and soldiers during these epic days."

Later in his speech, Mandela declared that in the days before the white men came to South Africa, "All men were free and equal and this was the foundation of government." He added, "There was much in such a society that was primitive and insecure and it certainly could never measure up to the needs of the present epoch. But in such a society are contained the seeds of evolutionary democracy in which none will be held in slavery or servitude, and in which poverty, want, and insecurity shall be no more. This is the inspiration which, even today, inspires me and my colleagues in our political struggle.''

The voice was that of Nelson Mandela, but the spirit of the speech was that of Tatu Joyi, and of Ngangelizwe and Ntombizodwa, and of all the other men and women who shared Mandela's African heritage.

# 3

# A Land of Beauty and Strife

AS A BOY, Nelson Mandela learned not just of his own Thembu ancestors but about many African leaders. There was Shaka, the Zulu king whose wars of conquest had thrown all of southern Africa into turmoil; Faku, the Pondo chieftain who had been pressured into signing a treaty with a British missionary that turned control of the Pondo lands over to the white men; Mqikela, Faku's son, who led his angry people in a rebellion against the treaty because they believed it was unfair; and Madikizela, head of the Ngutyana tribe, who married a daughter of Faku. Madikizela was the great-grandfather of Nomzamo Winnie Madikizela, who would one day become Nelson Mandela's wife.

These and other stories also made Nelson familiar with the folktales, religious beliefs, songs, and dances of his ancestors. He came to realize that the native black peoples of South Africa had possessed a complex and satisfying culture, rich in artistic achievement and spiritual values. When

23

the whites had made their way into the Transkei in the nineteenth century, they had dismissed the Africans as ignorant savages, simply because their way of life was so different from that of the Europeans. By labeling the black culture "primitive" and black people "inferior," the whites felt justified in taking over the land and imposing their own laws and customs on Africans.

One example of the kind of thinking that was typical of the white government can be found in a report prepared by the Department of Native Affairs, covering the years 1851 to 1902. In it, Nelson Mandela's people, the Thembu, are described as idle savages with *heathen*—that is, non-Christian—customs. No attempt was made by government officials to understand Thembu religious values or the significance of Thembu customs. Nelson was only one among the many black men and women in South Africa who grew up as second-class citizens in what had once been their own land.

The Republic of South Africa occupies the southern tip of the African continent. It consists of four provinces: Cape Province, the largest of the provinces, which includes the Transkei region where Nelson Mandela was born; the Transvaal, in the northeastern corner of the country; the Orange Free State, sandwiched between Cape Province and the Transvaal; and Natal, the smallest province, along the Indian Ocean coast at the eastern edge of the country. The independent black nation of Lesotho lies within South Africa's borders and is completely surrounded by South African territory.

In terms of natural resources, South Africa is one of the richest countries in Africa. Its mineral deposits are among the world's largest—at least 70 valuable minerals are mined in South Africa, including copper, chromium, manganese, iron ore, and coal. By far the most valuable are diamonds and gold. Diamonds were discovered in the Orange Free State in the 1860s, and gold was discovered in the Transvaal in the 1880s. Even after more than a century of mining, these deposits remain extensive.

The country also has productive farmland for growing corn, wheat, fruit, tobacco and other crops, and millions of acres of pasture for grazing sheep, goats, and cattle. Perhaps the only resources that are in short supply in South Africa are oil, which is purchased from other countries, and water, which is carefully conserved because rainfall tends to be low. Overall, South Africa is one of the world's more prosperous countries, and its standard of living is the highest in Africa. However, most of the country's wealth belongs to its 5 million white citizens, while the majority of its 28 million nonwhite people live in poverty.

In his 1962 courtroom speech, Nelson Mandela called South Africa "this beautiful land," and travelers throughout the centuries have spoken of its scenic beauty. One of the first was the English mariner Sir Francis Drake, who finished his sail around the world in 1580. After rounding the Cape of Good Hope near where Cape Town stands today, and gazing at the sparkling blue waters, white sandy beaches, and masses of flowering shrubs and vines, backed by the grandeur of Table Mountain, Drake declared, "This cape is a most stately thing and the fairest cape we saw in the whole circumference of the world."

In addition to the splendid scenery of the coast, South Africa contains stark deserts in the northwest and miles and miles of savannas, or grassy plains, in the northern and central parts of the country. Kruger National Park, one of the world's largest wild-game preserves, is located in the Transvaal. In the east there are lush palm and orchid forests.

As the southernmost country in Africa, South Africa is well below the equator, so it has a cooler, milder climate than many other African nations. It is temperate or subtropical rather than tropical. The weather is close to that of many European countries and the tropical diseases that are widespread in central Africa are rare there. For these reasons—and also because of its many natural resources—South Africa attracted more white settlers than other African countries colonized by Europeans.

The first colonists to arrive in South Africa, however, were not Europeans. They were Bantu-speaking Africans from the central part of Africa who, over a period of several centuries, migrated from their homelands to other parts of the continent. Bantu, or *abantu*, refers to a number of related ethnic or cultural groups, but is primarily a term describing related languages. There are almost 100 Bantu languages. The Bantu-speaking groups arrived in the area that is now South Africa around A.D. 300. They found the region already inhabited by a people called the Khoikhoi, who lived in small, roving family groups.

Contact between the Bantu and the Khoikhoi was sometimes peaceful, sometimes not. The Bantu killed some of the Khoikhoi and drove others north and west into the inhospitable deserts. But other groups of Khoikhoi lived harmoniously side by side with their Bantu neighbors and even intermarried with them. After a few centuries, Bantu-speakers had settled throughout what is now southeastern South Africa and were the dominant culture of the region. These were Nelson Mandela's ancestors.

There were many different groups among the Bantu colonists, and over time these groups split into still more subgroups. Chief among them were the Nguni, Zulu, Tsonga, Sotho, and Xhosa peoples. The Thembu are a later branch of the Xhosa. Each group developed a language of its own, although all of the languages retained their basic Bantu roots. Each isizwe also developed customs, beliefs, and art and craft forms of its own, unique but sill related to the larger *abantu* culture.

One cultural tool these peoples did not have was writing. Their histories, legends, and news were transmitted from village to village and from generation to generation by means of stories, songs, and poems that were recited instead of written in books. There were professional storytellers in every community, but everyone knew the most popular stories and songs. When he recounted tribal histories and old tales to his respectful listeners in the firelight at Mqekezweni, Tatu Joyi was part of this ancient and honorable oral tradition.

The Bantu brought many changes to southern Africa. Although the Khoikhoi people had been hunters and gatherers, the Bantu practiced farming and cattle herding. They knew how to smelt metal and how to make pottery. They also introduced large-scale settlement, building substantial villages and towns that were governed by sophisticated systems of chieftainships and priesthoods.

Some of these communities grew into powerful empires, such as the kingdom of Mapungubwe, which ruled the northern Transvaal between A.D. 1000 and 1500. The kings of Mapungubwe drew their wealth from gold and copper mines. They lived in a vast stone city on a hill above the Limpopo River, which forms part of South Africa's northern border today, and they carried on a brisk trade with Arabia and India. Centuries later, the European explorers who found the ruins of Mapungubwe and similar sites would dismiss as ridiculous the idea that black Africans could have built such sophisticated civilizations.

During the great era of European sea exploration, the Portuguese, Dutch, and English all sent ships along the coast of South Africa and around the Cape of Good Hope to the Indian Ocean. Table Bay became a sort of international post office—ships outward-bound from Europe would leave letters and messages in waterproof coverings under marked stones, and homeward-bound ships would pick them up to get news of home after several years' absence.

European colonization started in 1647, when the survivors of a Dutch shipwreck spent some months at the Cape. Upon their safe return to the Netherlands, they suggested that a settlement should be established at Table Bay. In 1652, the Dutch authorities sent about 60 settlers under the command of Jan van Riebeeck to build a fort there. That expedition was the start of the white presence in South Africa—and also of the troubled racial and ethnic relations that have plagued the country's history.

The Dutch settlers tried to make the local Khoikhoi work in their fields. The Khoikhoi were uncooperative and some were killed or imprisoned. One of these was Autshumayo, who escaped from Robben Island. So the Dutch imported black slaves from the east coast of Africa and Asian slaves from their holdings in Indonesia. The eventual intermingling of these slave populations with the Dutch and the surviving Khoikhoi produced a mixed-race population group that today's South African government calls the Coloured race.

The Dutch settlement grew larger. The settlers were thousands of miles distant from the Netherlands and gradually developed a new identity of their own. They called themselves Afrikaners, and they evolved a new language, based on Dutch, which they called Afrikaans. Rural Afrikaners came to be called Boers, from a Dutch word that means "farmer." Some Afrikaners stayed in or near the original settlement at Cape Town, but the Boers pushed farther and farther north and east into the interior, moving their families and servants with them in wagons. They did not know it, but they were on a collision course with another group of people on the move.

The *abantu* of the interior and the east coast were expanding and colonizing new areas themselves, moving steadily closer to the lands newly claimed by the white settlers. At the end of the eighteenth century, the movement of Boers and

Bantu met in the eastern central part of the country. The Xhosa, Sotho, and Nguni were the first groups to encounter the Boers. Unfortunately, the encounters were not peaceful ones.

The Boers intended to claim ownership of lands that the Bantu considered theirs by right, or at least open to all. The Boers fenced off their tracts of pastureland and the Xhosa and the Nguni swooped down on farmsteads in cattle raids, the usual form of skirmishing among Bantu isizwe. The whites reacted to the cattle raids by attacking the raiders and their villages, and soon the Boers and the Bantu were engaged in an all-out frontier war.

The Boers had other problems, too. England and the Netherlands were at war in Europe and the war spread to the Netherlands' African colony, which was seized by the British in 1795. British administrators took over the Cape area, but the Boers of the interior resisted British rule. Within a few years, however, England's control over the Cape colony was complete. British settlers began arriving in large numbers, bringing their language, customs, and culture with them.

Some of the rural Boers, determined to keep their own language and way of life intact, moved farther inland, away from British influence. But the greatest migration of Boers away from British rule took place between 1835 and 1843, when about 12,000 Afrikaners left the Cape to build new homes in the interior. This migration was called the Great Trek, and the Afrikaners who made it were the voortrekkers. They made the Great Trek to get away from the British, but they had to deal with angry Bantu groups along their route.

One of the most dramatic incidents of the Trek took place on the banks of the Ncome River, in present-day Natal province. A band of 500 Boer fighters held off an attack by 12,000 Zulu warriors, killing more than 3,000 of the attackers. Due to the superiority of rifles over spears, only three whites were killed. It is said that the river ran red with the blood of the fallen Zulus, and ever since it has been called Blood River. Their victory at Blood River did the Boers little good, however, as the British took control of Natal in 1843. The voortrekkers moved on, eventually settling throughout the present-day provinces of the Transvaal and the Orange Free State.

By the middle of the nineteenth century, South Africa consisted of two British colonies, the Cape Colony and Natal, two Boer republics, the Orange Free State and the Transvaal, and many small African states, which were eventually acquired by the British through conquest or treaty. Around this time, the British began bringing workers from India to work on sugar plantations in Natal. Many of these Indian workers sent for their families and settled permanently in South Africa. This was the beginning of South Africa's present-day Asian population.

The British and the Boers went to war in 1899. The bitterly fought war ended with a British victory in 1902, when the Orange Free State and the Transvaal surrendered and became British colonies. But the rift between whites of Boer descent and those of British descent persists in South Africa to this day.

In 1910, eight years before Mandela's birth, the four colonies were united as part of the British Empire and given the name the Union of South Africa. But unity did not prevail within the Union's borders. Not only were the Boers and the British still strongly at odds, but racial inequality was deeply entrenched. South Africans of Asian descent, led by Mahatma Gandhi, struggled without much success to gain equal rights with whites. People of mixed race, officially Coloureds, were discriminated against everywhere except in the Cape Colony, where they had secured a few rights.

Blacks, who were officially called Africans, were even more severely discriminated against than Asians or Coloureds. They were not allowed to own land outside tribal reservations and did not have the right to vote. In addition, most good jobs were closed to blacks, and educational opportunities for blacks were severely limited. In 1912, a group of African leaders responded to this state of affairs by forming an organization called the African National Congress (ANC) to work for black rights. The ANC became one of the largest and most powerful black equal rights groups in Africa.

Half a dozen years after the founding of the ANC, Nelson Mandela was born. The South Africa into which he came did not offer a very hopeful prospect to young Africans. Nelson could look forward to living in a society that would not let him vote and in which nearly all wealth and power were reserved for individuals who possessed something he would never have—a white skin. But, bad as things were for blacks in South Africa when Nelson Mandela was born in 1918, they would get worse.

# 4

# Journey to Johannesburg

WHILE NELSON MANDELA was learning about his African heritage from the stories of Tatu Joyi, his formal education was continuing as well. The school at Mqekezweni had only five grades, and in due time Nelson passed all his classes there. But according to Mandela's cousin Ntombizodwa, Chief Jongintaba did not consider that education a sufficient fulfillment of his responsibilities to Hendry Gadla's son. The chief drove young Nelson in his prized Ford automobile to the town of Qokolweni in the nearby Mqanduli district, where there was a higher-level elementary school. When Nelson graduated from this school, the family at Mqekezweni held a celebration in his honor, slaughtering a sheep for a special feast.

When the celebration was over, it was time to make plans for high school. Nelson was to attend a Methodist high school called Clarkebury in Engcobo, one of the major towns of the Umtata district. Wearing a brand-new school uniform and a pair of shiny leather shoes that had been bought for him by Jongintaba, Nelson once again climbed into the chief's Ford V-8 and was driven to his new school.

At some time during Nelson's high-school years, when he was sixteen, he took part in a traditional tribal ceremony that marked his coming of age as a man among his people. This ritual took place on the banks of a small river called the Bashee, which had been part of Thembu territory for centuries. Nelson calls the ceremony "circumcision school." Although details of individual rites are not made public, it is known that young people throughout much of Africa have traditionally taken part in circumcision ceremonies in their middle teens. Generally, all the young men of the village or community who are close together in age are circumcised at the same time. They spend a period of time—from overnight to about a month—living in isolation from the rest of the community, often in a special house near a river.

During this time, the elders of the tribe instruct them in the responsibilities they will share once they are regarded as men and no longer children. At the end of the period of isolation, the circumcision is performed. Afterward, the men are welcomed back into the community with a celebration that includes feasting, singing, and dancing. The ceremony was an important link to the Thembu past. Mandela proudly notes that it occurred at "the place where many of my ancestors were circumcised."

Although he was now an adult in the eyes of the African community, Mandela still had to complete his formal education. He finished his schooling at

Clarkebury. Another celebration took place in his honor at Mqekezweni, and this one was even larger than before, for it was a double celebration. Not only had Mandela graduated from Clarkebury, but it had been decided that he was to go to college.

In 1938, there were few choices in South Africa for black students who wanted a university education. In Cape Province, there was only one choice, Fort Hare, a blacks-only university located near the city of Alice. Mandela was admitted to Fort Hare, and Jongintaba proudly took his nephew to a tailor and had a three-piece suit made for him so that he would be properly dressed for his classes. All of Mqekezweni was proud of Nelson Mandela: "We thought," recalls Ntombizodwa, "there could never be anyone smarter than him at Fort Hare."

Mandela enrolled at Fort Hare in 1939. There he made a number of new friends. One of the first people he met was Kaiser Matanzima, a Thembu who was Mandela's nephew, although the two were about the same age. Matanzima was a fun-loving companion, and the two considered themselves quite sophisticated and stylish. Matanzima, who later became a chief and went on to become a high-ranking official in the government of the Transkei, recalls, "The two of us were very handsome young men and all the women wanted us."

Mandela recalls that they developed a passion for ballroom dancing and spent hours learning to waltz and fox-trot. They wanted to show off their skill at a dance hall called Ntselamanzi, which was the social center for the well-to-do and well-educated Africans of the area. Unfortunately, however, the dance hall was off-limits to students. Says

35

Mandela, "Undaunted, we sneaked out of our dormitories and presented ourselves at Ntselamanzi. There was always the chance we might bump into one of our masters [that is, professors]. We took that chance."

One night, Mandela saw a particularly attractive woman and invited her to dance. As they were foxtrotting across the floor, he was horrified to discover that she was the wife of one of his professors. Looking across the dance floor, he saw the lady's husband and another professor eyeing him coldly. He apologized and withdrew in embarrassment. To his great relief neither of the men ever mentioned the matter.

Mandela's life at Fort Hare was not all fox-trots and light-hearted escapades, however. In fact, his time at college saw the birth of his lifelong commitment to political activism. He made the acquaintance of some fellow students who were interested in political philosophy. Together they spent hours discussing the injustices of white rule in South Africa and speculating on how the lives of blacks might be improved. Among these friends were Oliver Tambo and Congress Mbata. Both were to play important roles in Mandela's political life in the years to come.

In 1940, while they were still at Fort Hare, Tambo and Mandela got into trouble over political action—a prelude to the much greater trouble that each would encounter later in life. A dispute arose between the students and the school authorities. According to Ntombizodwa, it had to do with the quality of the food that was provided to the students. Hoping to end the protest, the authorities greatly reduced the rights and powers of the Stu-

dents' Representative Council. Several students—
with Mandela and Tambo among them—then tried
to organize a student boycott of the Council. They
encouraged the students to ignore the Council and
form new organizations to negotiate with the college officials. The authorities regarded the boycott
as a form of disruptive agitation and suspended
the agitators, including Tambo and Mandela. The
result was that after less than two years of college,
Mandela was sent home.

Chief Jongintaba was not pleased to see his
nephew return home in disgrace. Knowing that if
Mandela apologized to the college authorities and
promised to behave himself in the future he would
be readmitted, Jongintaba urged Mandela to go
back to Fort Hare in a suitably apologetic manner.
But Mandela could be extremely stubborn when
he wanted to be. He felt no shame or disgrace at
his suspension from college because he believed
that he had acted rightly. He knew that, if necessary, he would do the same thing over again, for
he had come to believe that it was every person's
right to organize for free expression. This principle
has remained with him ever since.

So Mandela remained in Mqekezweni. He had a
home there for as long as he wanted it, and he
could easily have made a place for himself in local
tribal politics. There was nothing to prevent him
from marrying, starting a small farm of his own,
and settling down—nothing except his own burning desire to finish his education and to get involved in what was happening in the larger world
outside the horizons of Mqekezweni.

By this time, the Union of South Africa was an
independent nation. It had declared its indepen-

dence from the British in 1934, although it remained part of the British Commonwealth of Nations, a political and economic union that included Great Britain and many of its former colonies and territories around the world. Now World War II was raging in Europe, and many Africans sensed that the aftermath of the war would bring changes to Africa. Despite his respect for tribal tradition, Mandela wanted a different kind of life for himself. He wanted to study law and recapture the exciting spirit of political involvement that he had shared with Oliver Tambo and Congress Mbata at Fort Hare. For these reasons, he began to think about leaving Mqekezweni. At this point, his uncle provided him with yet another reason to leave.

Chief Jongintaba decided that it was high time that his 23-year-old nephew was married. According to custom, it was not uncommon for marriages to be arranged by the parents or guardians of young men and women. Jongintaba therefore selected a suitable bride for Mandela and paid the traditional *lobola*, or bride-price, which is a gift of money or cattle from the groom's family to the bride's. When it came to getting the prospective groom to agree to the wedding, however, the chief discovered that Mandela had a mind of his own.

Mandela loved and respected his uncle and hated to disobey him. Yet he was completely unwilling to go along with the arranged marriage. "He loved me very much and looked after me as diligently as my father had," says Mandela of Jongintaba. "But he was no democrat and did not think it worthwhile to consult me about a wife." The girl Jongintaba had selected did not appeal to Mandela. While the village was preparing for the wedding, the groom took matters into his own hands and fled.

He was accompanied in his flight from Mqeke-zweni by his cousin Justice Mtirara. The two young men agreed that they should make for Johannesburg, the largest city in South Africa. Located in the Transvaal, Johannesburg was a booming, bustling center of mining and industry. Mandela and Mtirara were sure that they could find work there, but they would need funds to reach Johannesburg. They stole two oxen from Jongintaba's cattle herd, sold them to a local trader, and made off with the cash.

"We used the money to dash to Johannesburg," Mandela recalled years later, "and after clearing many hurdles, we eventually reached the Golden City." Johannesburg could well be called South Africa's Golden City. Located in the heart of the gold-mining district called the Rand, it was the financial capital of the country. When Mandela and Mtirara arrived on its streets in 1941, Johannesburg was growing by leaps and bounds. Africans from around the country flooded into the city, looking for work. The war was intensifying in Europe, and South Africa's mines and factories were pouring forth material to aid Great Britain and its allies. There was plenty of work, but most of the workers had great difficulty finding a place to live.

Johannesburg itself was off-limits to Africans, who could work within the city but could not live there. Blacks had to live in the various nonwhite suburbs and townships that formed a ragged ring around the outer edge of the city. The principal black townships then were Sophiatown, Newclare, Martindale, and Alexandra. They consisted of row upon row of single-story brick dwellings that had been hastily erected and resembled army barracks. So crowded were these townships that sometimes forty or more people had to share a single water faucet or toilet and almost no one had a room to himself or herself.

Yet the traditional support structure of the African extended family was at work even in these difficult conditions. Newcomers could often find lodging with their relatives, and people with family or tribal connections helped one another.

Mandela and Mtirara discovered the strength of the tribal bond when they presented themselves to the only person they knew in Johannesburg, a man who had been a member of Chief Jongintaba's court and was now an overseer, or foreman, at the Crown Mines. The overseer considered it both a responsibility and an honor to find jobs at the mine for two members of the chief's family. He secured one opening for a *mabhalane*, or trainee clerk, and one for a mine policeman, or security guard. The clerk's position paid more and had higher status than the policeman's, so it went to Mtirara, the older of the two young men. Mandela was made a policeman, but he was assured that he would be given the next clerkship that became available. All in all, it looked as though the two runaways were off to a fair start.

Within a few days, however, their fortunes underwent a drastic change. Chief Jongintaba had been very displeased that Mandela refused to go through with the planned marriage and even more displeased that the two young men had run away. Worse, the theft of his oxen had been a serious violation of the tribal laws of property and respect.

He sent men out to track down the runaways.
When he learned that they had gone to Johannesburg and were working at Crown Mines, he tele-
graphed to the overseer and told him to dismiss
Mtirara and Mandela and send them home. Their
careers at Crown were over.

Mtirara returned home, but Mandela managed
to persuade Jongintaba that he should remain in
Johannesburg, where he could study law and pur-
sue his dream of becoming an attorney. The chief
agreed that this would be a suitable fulfillment of
his responsibility to Hendry Gadla, Mandela's dead
father. So Mandela stayed in the Golden City. He
knew that he had chosen a difficult path, but he
also knew that Jongintaba supported his decision
and would help him if needed.

# 5

# Family Man, Young Politician

MANDELA'S FIRST TASK in Johannesburg was to find a new job. Before long he found work in a real-estate office. The salary he earned was painfully low. It allowed him to live, but he said later that the year he spent working as a housing agent was "the most difficult time of my life." Out of his meager salary he had to pay bus fare every day to travel back and forth between Johannesburg, where he worked, and Alexandra Township, where he had found lodging with a family. He paid for his room and board, but the landlord and his wife treated him with great kindness, allowing him to pay his rent late if he had money problems and always giving him a big lunch, free of charge, on Sundays.

A little while later Mandela boarded with a minister of the Anglican Church named the Reverend Mabuto, who also lived in Alexandra Township. The minister and his wife made Mandela feel very welcome, although the minister's wife had rather strict ideas about relationships between people of different ethnic backgrounds. She insisted that Mandela should date only Xhosa girls.

Mandela's own outlook on ethnic matters had become more broad-minded. At high school and at Fort Hare he had gotten to know students from different African tribes. He was proud of the fact that he had begun to think beyond ethnic limitations. In the years to come, the scope of Mandela's friendships would broaden to include not just blacks from other tribal backgrounds but also Asians, Coloureds, and whites, leading him to seek equal rights not just for black Africans, but for all.

The first friends he made in Johannesburg, however, were fellow Xhosas. He met a young nursing student who lived nearby in Alexandra Township. She was impressed with this energetic, bright young man fresh from the Transkei who seemed ambitious but who, she sensed, was not certain how to go about achieving his goals. This woman introduced Mandela to a friend who was also studying nursing at Johannesburg General Hospital. The friends' name as Albertina Totiwe, and she in turn introduced Mandela to her fiancé, whose name was Walter Sisulu. Their first meeting was the start of a lifelong friendship and political partnership that has survived years of turmoil and imprisonment, and still flourishes today.

Walter Sisulu was the son of a Xhosa woman from the Transkei and a white man who had worked as foreman of a road-building crew there. The foreman did not marry MaSisulu, as she was called, and after he left her she took their two small children to Johannesburg and found work as a washerwoman to pay for their high-school educations. By the time he met Nelson Mandela, Walter

Sisulu was studying law. He lived with his mother in Orlando, a black neighborhood that was closer to Johannesburg than Alexandra. It was part of the area that would soon be called South-West Township, or Soweto. Today Soweto is a vast African suburb of Johannesburg.

Walter Sisulu and Nelson Mandela liked each other immediately. Walter suggested that Mandela should move into the Sisulu home in Orlando, and Mandela accepted with pleasure. Not only would the move bring him closer to his work in Johannesburg, it would give him the opportunity to spend time with his new friend. He discovered that Sisulu was interested in political matters and had many acquaintances in the growing group of politically active Africans in Johannesburg.

Anton Lembede, who wrote, "A new spirit of African Nationalism, or Africanism, is pervading through and stirring African society," was a leader among them. Jordan Ngubane, M. T. Morane, and H.I.E. Dhlomo, editors of black newspapers who spread the idea of black nationalism among their readers, were also among them. Mandela also renewed his friendship with Oliver Tambo and Congress Mbata, who were living in Johannesburg. He found another old friend in Victor Mbobo, one of his high-school teachers who was now part of the black political scene.

During his first months in the city, Mandela was constantly surprised by contrasts between rural and urban ways of life. He felt like a country bumpkin on one occasion when he purchased a piece of beef in a food shop and asked one of his landlady's daughters to cook it for him. To his embarrassment, she laughed and told him that it did not need to be cooked because it was smoked meat, something that he had never seen. Another time he went to visit a man who had been one of his high-school teachers.

"He was a good qualified teacher and a graduate," recalls Mandela, "married to an equally well-qualified nurse." He found their house shut up tight and smelled a terrible odor of old-fashioned herbal medicines coming from inside. A traditional tribal healer, or *inyanga*, was at work in the house, burning leaves and reciting traditional incantations. Just then the man's wife stepped out of the house and said that her husband was ill and that she believed that he had been bewitched—by Mandela himself!

"I was very troubled," Mandela says, "and went straight to Anton Lembede and told him of my experience. He only laughed."

Mandela soon got over his culture shock. He managed to obtain his bachelor of arts degree in 1942. His friend Sisulu congratulated him with the gift of a new suit for the graduation ceremony. Mandela then enrolled in the law program at Witwatersrand University. At about this time, with Sisulu's help, he got a job as a clerk in the law office of Witkin, Sidelsky, and Edelman. He worked for attorney Lazer Sidelsky, a white man who, as Mandela says, "practically became an elder brother to me." In 1964, Mandela wrote, "To Mr. Sidelsky, I will always be indebted."

While working for Sidelsky, Mandela learned that it was possible for him to form bonds of respect and even of affection with whites. But not all of his experiences with white coworkers were pleasant ones. On his first day on the job, the senior typist, who was white, politely told Mandela that the office workers were not prejudiced and that he would be allowed to take his coffee break with the whites. Then he was informed that a special cup had been purchased for him to use, so that he would not use a cup that might be used by a white worker on another day.

Another unpleasant experience involved a white typist in the office who sometimes did work for Mandela. One day a white client walked in and discovered the typist taking dictation from Mandela. Embarrassed to be seen working for a black man, the typist quickly took some change from her purse and ordered Mandela to go pick up her shampoo from the drugstore as though he were an errand boy. Such treatment only served to drive home to Mandela the knowledge that racial prejudice was deeply ingrained in many white South Africans, even in some of those who believed themselves to be open-minded.

Race, in fact, was and is the dominant fact of life for all South Africans. From the beginning of white settlement in South Africa, relations between groups had taken place on a footing of racial hostility and separateness. As time passed, the nonwhite peoples remained politically and economically overpowered by the whites. South Africa's government and social structure were defined by racist thinking.

In its most basic form, racism is the notion that the physical characteristics that distinguish one group of people from another—skin color being the most obvious of these characteristics—are somehow directly related to such qualities as intelligence, behavior, character, and personality.

Genetic differences, such as skin color, do occur but it is now known that they have nothing to do with performance or individual potential. In fact, many scientists feel that the term *race* is not appropriate for use in the discussion of human beings, because the word seems to mean whatever a given society wants it to mean. Some individuals who would be considered black in the United States would be considered white in Brazil, for example.

In South Africa, however, racist thinking became the basis of a whole society. In the twentieth century, the word *apartheid* (Afrikaans for "apartness") came to be used to describe the way whites thought about race. Social, religious, and political thinkers—mostly in the provinces of the Transvaal and the Orange Free State, where many Afrikaners lived—developed several apartheid theories.

One version, put forth by the Dutch Reformed Church and the government's South African Bureau of Racial Affairs (SABRA), held that the various "races" of South Africa were technically equal but should not be forced or even allowed to merge. These theorists felt that each race should develop separately, and their goal was to divide South Africa into completely separate black and white states. A more extreme version of apartheid theory claimed not only that the "races" are distinct from one another but that the white race is fundamentally superior to all others, especially to the African. The whites who held this philosophy believed that it was the destiny of nonwhite people to serve the whites and that nonwhites were not capable of governing themselves.

The philosophy of apartheid, rooted as it was in

several centuries of white domination in South Africa, gained believers yearly, particularly after World War II, when many European colonies in Africa shook off their white, colonial administrations and became independent, black-ruled states. Most South African whites were determined not to let that happen to "their" country. Those who preached the theory of apartheid held it up as a shield to protect white privileges. For educated Africans like Nelson Mandela, apartheid was a weight that unjustly held them down.

Mandela went on with the business of making his own way in the big city. His friendship with Walter Sisulu not only brought him a new job and a new home, it brought him romance as well. A cousin of Sisulu's arrived in Johannesburg a few years before Mandela did. She was a nursing student named Ntoko Evelyn Mase, and she was from Engcobo in the Transkei, not far from where Mandela grew up. Both of her parents died during her childhood, and she was raised by her siblings. In 1939, Evelyn and one of her brothers came to live with Walter Sisulu's mother, MaSisulu, who was the sister of their father's first wife. In typical *abantu* fashion, MaSisulu extended a warm welcome to the two orphans and made them as comfortable as possible in her home. When Evelyn's brother married and obtained a house of his own in Orlando, Evelyn moved in with the newlyweds. She continued to pay regular visits to the Sisulu home, however, and it was there that she met Mandela in 1944.

At that time, he was a tall, broad-shouldered man of twenty-six. He kept fit and muscular by amateur boxing, and he was considered very handsome, with a trim mustache and a broad smile. Evelyn was immediately attracted to him. "I think I loved him the first time I saw him," she says. "The Sisulus had many friends. They were such genial, generous people and Walter had lots of friends who came to their home, but there was something very special about Nelson."

Soon after that first meeting, Mandela and Evelyn were dating steadily. Before long, Mandela decided that he was ready to get married—to the bride of his own choice, this time, and not to one chosen for him by his uncle. He proposed to Evelyn and she joyously accepted. Evelyn's brother gave the couple his blessing and within weeks they were married at the Native Commissioner's Court in Johannesburg.

Mandela and his new wife could not afford to give the traditional wedding feast for their friends and relatives. Indeed, they were nearly always short of money. Mandela was studying toward his law degree and worked only part-time, and Evelyn's income from nursing was their primary source of funds. They could not find a house to rent, so they lived with Evelyn's married sister and her husband. "There was no question of paying toward board and lodging," Evelyn says. "They were family."

In 1945, the Mandelas' first child, a boy, was born. They named him Madiba Thembikele; he was called Thembi. Mandela surprised Evelyn by showing up at the hospital with an armload of nightgowns for her and new clothes for the baby. When the mother and baby came home, Evelyn was touched to discover that Mandela had managed to buy a fine cot for Thembi. After Thembi's birth, the housing authorities gave the Mandelas a two-room house of their own in Orlando. Later, in 1947, they obtained a three-room house, also in Orlando.

Just as family members had offered hospitality to Mandela and to Evelyn, now they were able to take care of relatives in turn. Mandela's sister Leabie came from Qunu to live with them. As her older brother, Mandela was responsible for her education and saw to it that she was enrolled at Orlando High School.

The Mandelas' second child was born in 1948. They named the baby girl Makaziwe. She became ill and died at the age of nine months. The following year, Mandela received a letter from Qunu, telling him that his mother, Nosekeni Fanny Mandela, was feeling unwell and needed medical treatment. He sent money so that she could come to Johannesburg to see a special doctor. Nosekeni Fanny stayed on in Johannesburg and made her home with her son and his wife. She helped with the housework and took care of Thembi while Evelyn was at work. Mandela's family responsibilities increased once again in 1950, when his second son was born. This boy was named Makgatho. The couple's third and last child was born in 1954. She was named Makaziwe, but called by the nickname Maki.

During the late 1940s, as Evelyn describes, the Mandelas "settled into a happy, crowded family." Nelson was very busy and followed a strict schedule. He got up at dawn every day, jogged a few miles to keep fit, ate a light breakfast, and was off to the day's work. Evelyn remembers that he enjoyed doing the family shopping and giving the baby boys their evening baths. He even took over the role of cook once in a while. Friends and relatives from the Transkei often stayed with the Mandelas for weeks or even months.

"We made them feel that the house was their own and they had every right to it," says Evelyn. "We made the beds on the floor when there were too many of us. We never felt that there wasn't enough room. Somehow there was always room."

Kaiser Matanzima, with whom Mandela had become friendly at Fort Hare, was one of the most frequent guests. Evelyn became active in the nursing union, along with Oliver Tambo's fiancée, Adelaide Tsukudu. The union hoped to protect the rights of nurses and to gain equal pay for black nurses. Mandela was happy to see his wife getting involved in political activity, for by this time politics had come to occupy a great deal of his own time and energy.

Mandela's political life began to take shape soon after he met Walter Sisulu. By introducing him to a wide circle of African friends who were politically active, Sisulu showed Mandela how he could channel his own feelings and beliefs into actions. In 1944, Mandela joined the African National Congress. The ANC had been in existence for more than thirty years. Mandela's own father, Hendry Gadla, had been a member. Yet Mandela, Sisulu, and some of their friends felt the ANC was not doing enough to promote African values. They wanted an organization that would not only try to win concessions from the whites but would also encourage African culture and African solidarity, particularly among young people. They decided to carry out their ideas through a new organization within the ANC. A few months later, a handful of men met at the Bantu Men's Social Center in Johannesburg and formed the ANC Youth League. Among the founders were Sisulu, Mandela, Anton Lembede, Oliver Tambo, Congress Mbata, Victor Mbobo, and Jordan Ngubane. Lembede was elected president of the Youth League. Mandela and Sisulu were elected to the League's executive committee.

The founders and members of the Youth League were Africanists. Their philosophy was that the blacks of South Africa should dominate the other races politically and culturally because blacks dramatically outnumbered the other races and had historical rights to the land. Some of the Africanists went so far as to say that there should be no place in South Africa for whites, Asians, or Coloureds. Yet while Mandela was strongly attracted to Africanism because of the high value it placed upon his own *abantu* heritage, he also began to be exposed to other points of view.

In his law classes at Witwatersrand University, he met Coloured, Asian, and white students who shared his belief that South Africa's treatment of its black people was appallingly unjust, but who called for an open, multiracial society as the answer to the problem. Gradually, as his acquaintance with non-Africans deepened, Mandela's own philosophy evolved from the Africanist ideal of black supremacy to a more tolerant, multiracial democratic ideal. He became a member and later an officer of a group called the International Club, which existed to give members the opportunity to meet members of other races in a social setting, unconnected with either business or politics.

One white member of the International Club, an insurance agent named Gordon Bruce, became a particularly close friend. Mandela recalls that once Bruce called him and asked him, as a favor, to give his wife a ride home from work. Mandela went to downtown Johannesburg and met Ursula Bruce, who was blind. She rested her hand on his arm as he led her to the car. "If looks could kill I would have been dead that day," he said later. "I had the feeling that the scores of whites who passed us by were ready to spit on us. A kaffir boy escorting a white woman!" (*Kaffir* is an uncomplimentary term used by some white South Africans to refer to blacks; it is actually an Arabic word that means "infidel" or "unbeliever" and was used by Arab traders along the African coast centuries ago to describe non-Muslims.)

From his Asian friends—mostly of Indian and Pakistani descent—Mandela learned about the method of passive resistance to authority that had been pioneered by Mahatma Gandhi. He received a personal lesson in resistance to injustice one day when he and three Indian fellow students tried to ride a bus together. At that time, there were separate buses for whites and nonwhites. Asians and Coloureds could often get away with riding on "Whites Only" buses. Blacks, however, could not. The four men got on a bus reserved for whites. It had traveled barely a block when the conductor said to Mandela's companions, "Hey, you are not allowed to bring a kaffir aboard." The conductor added, pointing to Mandela, "That kaffir there," and ordered Mandela off the bus.

Mandela refused to leave. At the next stop, the conductor summoned a policeman, who told the

Indians to tell Mandela to leave the bus. They refused, and the policeman arrested one of them, Ismail Meer. The policeman took Mandela aside and suggested that if he made a statement against the Indian, he would be dismissed without charges. Mandela replied indignantly that the policeman had better arrest him, too.

The case was brought to trial in front of a magistrate the next day. Ismail Meer, the defendant, came into the courtroom with his fellow students and with his attorney, Bram Fischer. A liberal white lawyer who was a member of South Africa's Communist Party, Fischer also happened to be the son of a very important official in the Orange Free State. As a result, the magistrate treated Fischer and his client with great courtesy and ruled in favor of Meer. But the fundamental problem remained unsolved, for Mandela and his friends knew that they would encounter the same hostility if they tried to ride a whites-only bus again.

In the ANC Youth League, Mandela's closest friends were Alter Sisulu and Oliver Tambo. Like them, Mandela approved of the strikes and other protest actions that were being organized around the country by the Communist Party and by the Indians, but he also felt that the ANC should play a leading role in the protest against white injustice. He observed that there were many rivalries and disputes among ANC members, or between the ANC and other organizations, such as the Communist Party. He knew that these rifts could only weaken the overall protest movement. In the future, he would call repeatedly for unity among all those who fought against white supremacy.

Part of Mandela's political education in the

Youth League involved public speaking. He became a great admirer of A. P. Mda, a fellow member of the executive committee of the League, who was noted for his clear thinking and his well-organized, finely phrased speeches. Mandela began to develop his own speech-making skills, learning to marshal his thoughts in good order and to express them in crisp, memorable words. This skill became especially important in 1947. In that year, Anton Lembede fell ill suddenly and died. He was succeeded as president of the Youth League by Mda, and Mandela was elected to fill the post of general secretary, which Mda had held. This was Mandela's first step toward a position of leadership within the ANC.

His responsibilities took up a great deal of time. One of his principal tasks was to get the Youth League established nationally by encouraging ANC members to form branches in other cities and provinces. He was often on the road, traveling for days at a time to meet with ANC officials and new Youth League members around the country. The work was demanding, but it gave Mandela the opportunity to get to know black leaders in all parts of the country and for them to get to know him.

By 1948, Mandela had accomplished much in the seven years since he had stolen two oxen and run away to Johannesburg. He had earned a college degree and made a good start at the study of law. He had fallen in love, married, and started a family. And he had found an outlet for his political activism in the ANC, where he had been elected to an important position. But 1948 was a crucial year not just in Nelson Mandela's life, but in the history of South Africa.

Racial unrest had been growing stronger for several years and questions about the right of the white government to suppress the other races were being asked more and more loudly around the world. The South African government was particularly unhappy about a situation that had developed in the United Nations in 1946 and 1947. The Indian population of South Africa resented laws that barred Indians from buying new property in Durban, a city in Natal Province where many Indians lived. The government of India, which was sympathetic to people of Indian descent living in other nations, attacked South Africa's racial discrimination in the United Nations General Assembly. As a result the United Nations passed the first of many resolutions expressing condemnation of South Africa's racist policies.

Even some white South Africans began to say that the government should change its policies to give more rights to nonwhites. A much greater number of whites, however, felt that even more stern measures were necessary to keep the other races subservient. One political party in particular adopted the philosophy of apartheid to bolster continued white supremacy. It was called the Nationalist Party and it had many members in the Transvaal and the Orange Free State. Many Nationalists were Afrikaners who continued to feel, as their Boer ancestors had felt, that South Africa must be a white man's country.

As the 1948 elections approached, race relations deteriorated further. Angry Indians were demanding equal rights in Natal. Elsewhere in the country, Africans were banding together in greater numbers than ever before under the banners of the

ANC, the Youth League, the Communist Party, and other organizations that promised to fight for their rights. Even the Coloured South Africans, who had long had a better relationship with the whites than either the Asians or the Africans, were beginning to call for change. At the same time, the large segment of the white population that shared the views of the Nationalist Party was saying that the Africans, Asians, and Coloureds should be more firmly segregated than ever.

The Nationalist Party entered many candidates in the elections. Tension built as election day drew near, hanging over the country like a thick, dark cloud. The outcome of the elections would change the country forever. Finally the day came when South Africa's voters—that is, its *white* citizens—went to the polls. Across the country, on isolated Boer farmsteads and in crowded African townships, in the glittering financial district of Johannesburg and in the dusty villages of the Transkei, people gathered around radios, waiting for the election results. When the votes had been counted, the word went out: The Nationalists had swept to power. They now controlled the prime ministership and the legislature. South Africa had passed a turning point.

# 6

# Apartheid and Resistance

THE GOAL OF the Nationalist Party was simple: to maintain white supremacy in South Africa, although the nonwhite population greatly outnumbered the white population. The Nationalists hoped to achieve this goal through a system of tough, new apartheid laws, which were put in force in the 1950s.

One of the Nationalists' first steps was to pass the Population Registration Act in 1950. Under this law, every South African was classified as a member of one of four races: white, Coloured, Asian, or African. An individual's racial status was determined at birth and was the single most important fact of his or her life. Throughout the 1950s, other laws were welded onto the structure of apartheid. The races were educated separately and could not intermarry, join the same political parties or unions, worship in the same churches, live in the same neighborhoods, or even use the same drinking fountains, movie theaters, or hospitals. Africans and Asians could not vote. Coloureds were given a limited form of representation in the government, since they were permitted to vote for white candidates.

Some of the apartheid laws were simply the continuation of earlier laws, but others were newly restrictive. For example, African men had always been required to carry "passes" if they wanted to go back and forth from nonwhite to white areas, as many of them did going to and from work every day. Under the Nationalists, the pass laws were made more strict and were extended to women. A curfew for nonwhites was enforced, making it illegal for them to move about in the streets or public places after 11 P.M.

The most sweeping aspect of apartheid policy introduced by the Nationalists concerned geography. Previous governments had established certain areas throughout the country as tribal "homelands." These were essentially reservations and most rural blacks lived in these separate areas. Under the Nationalists, the existing homelands were restructured into ten districts called Bantustans, or black states, one for each of the major African ethnic groups, which were defined by the government with little regard for the true nature of tribal relationships. The total area of the Bantustans amounted to less than 13 percent of the country and, as critics of apartheid quickly pointed out, included a great deal of barren, unproductive land. The 87 percent reserved for whites contained all of the country's natural resources and rich farmland.

Africans who held jobs in the white areas were permitted to live there in segregated townships, such as Soweto, but all others were required to settle on the Bantustans to which the government had assigned them. Many Africans were uprooted and relocated, sometimes forcibly, to the new Bantustans, which had little or nothing in the way of schools, medical facilities, stores, or even water supplies.

The Nationalists' idea was that the Africans would be permitted to govern their own affairs within the Bantustans—under supervision by the central white government, of course. It would thus seem as though blacks were being given just what they had been asking for—self-government. In reality, however, the Bantustans were nothing more than puppet states, weak and completely dependent economically upon the central government. Allowing Africans to run the Bantustans was simply a new way of denying them full citizenship in the country as a whole.

A rift developed between those Africans who went along with the government's Bantustan policy and those who opposed it. The former felt that even a little bit of very limited power was better than nothing at all. The latter scorned the Bantustans because they sought full citizenship and full participation in the central government. This conflict escalated into violence in many areas and continues to divide South Africa's blacks today. It touched Mandela's life when the Transkei was made a Bantustan. His kinsman and old friend Kaiser Matanzima, a chief of the Madiba clan, cooperated with the Nationalist government and was given a high post in the Bantustan administration. Mandela, who despised the Bantustan program as an attempt to cheat the Africans out of their rights,

"Apartheid" is the Afrikaaner word for "apartness," which means forcing people from different racial groups to live apart from each other. Schools, universities, hospitals, parks, buses, and even beaches were segregated. On this beach in the city of Durban, a sign in three languages—English, Afrikaaner and Xhosa—warns that only white people are allowed here.

admitted with sorrow that he viewed Matanzima as a traitor.

While the Nationalists were forging the cage of apartheid, Mandela and other angry Africans intensified their resistance to racial oppression. The cloud of foreboding that had seemed to gather over the nation at the time of the 1948 elections grew more ominous. Many whites feared that the tension would erupt in a bloodbath. Some whites bought guns and turned their homes into fortresses. Others, no longer willing to live in a country that openly embraced racism as an institutional policy, emigrated to other parts of the world. The 1950s were a decade of increasing militancy for Africans in general and for the ANC in particular. And as the decade progressed, Mandela became more and more a leader.

In 1949, Walter Sisulu was elected secretary general of the ANC and Oliver Tambo was elected to its executive committee. Mandela was later added to the committee. In 1951, the Youth League joined an Asian political organization called the Indian Congress in calling for a national workers' strike on June 26, the anniversary of the day the Nationalists came to power. Mandela was given the responsibility of heading the planning committee. In the months before the strike he crisscrossed the country, urging ANC branches and dozens of other groups to support the strike, which he claimed would demonstrate the economic power of the nonwhite workers.

The strike was moderately successful, and Mandela noted that a great many Asians supported it by staying away from work, especially in Durban. This reinforced the shift in his political thinking from a strongly Africanist point of view to a non-racial one that envisioned unity among anti-apartheid groups of all races.

The ANC decided to follow the strike with a new form of resistance in 1952. Together with the Indian Congress, ANC leaders planned what they called the Defiance of Unjust Laws Campaign. Their idea was that anti-apartheid volunteers would deliberately break selected apartheid laws, such as the pass law and the curfew. The jails and courts would be jammed and the protest would call attention to the futility of the laws. Mandela was appointed volunteer-in-chief and once again took responsibility for supervising the national campaign, which was scheduled to start on June 26.

On that day, bands of African and Indian resisters filed into streets across the land and systematically violated the apartheid laws. Walter Sisulu led a group that entered an African township without the required permits. All were arrested. Mandela coached a group of fifty African resisters in the techniques of passive resistance. When the clock struck 11 P.M., he led them out into the street in violation of the curfew. The police bundled Mandela and the other volunteers into vans and carried them off to prison. Mandela spent a night or so in jail before being released on bail. The charges against him were later dropped.

The Defiance of Unjust Laws Campaign continued. It spread to Natal and the Cape. New recruits joined the ANC in droves. Mandela experienced the government's reaction firsthand early one July morning. He was asleep at home when he woke suddenly to the sound of fists pounding on the door. The house was surrounded by police, who

63

had swooped down in a night raid on the homes of about twenty African activists. All spent a few days in jail. In the years to come, Mandela and his family would grow accustomed to such sudden wakings and surprise raids.

During the campaign, the ANC experienced some changes. Albert Luthuli, a chief of the Makholweni, was elected its president. Mandela was elected president of the Transvaal branch of the ANC. The ANC leaders decided to end the campaign after riots broke out in the Cape Province, where more than a dozen people, white and black, were killed. By that time, 8,577 volunteers had deliberately broken apartheid laws. The government responded to the riots by banning 52 activists, including Luthuli and Mandela. This was Mandela's first experience of being banned; it was not his last.

"Banning" is one of the methods used by the Nationalist government to suppress the anti-apartheid movement. A banned individual is not allowed to be present in any group of more than three people, no matter who they are or what they are doing. Furthermore, a banned person may not be quoted in the newspapers or on television and his or her words may not be published. Violations of a banning order can result in swift imprisonment. Sometimes banning is combined with house arrest, in which the banned person's movements are strictly limited. Banning is used to isolate political activists from their followers. It is like a prison without walls.

Organizations and publications can also be banned. The South African government banned the Communist Party in 1950, and an anti-apartheid newspaper called *The Guardian* was also banned. The Nationalists were to use banning many times against Nelson Mandela, his family, and other anti-apartheid activists, black and white.

Because Mandela was banned, he was unable to appear at the meeting of the Transvaal ANC at which his election to the presidency of the organization was announced. Instead, he wrote a speech that was read aloud to the convention by another ANC member. In it, he told the listeners that freedom and racial equality were inevitable, but that blacks would have "no easy walk to freedom."

Mandela's first ban expired in 1953, but he was banned again almost immediately for antigovernment protests. The new ban was for two years. Mandela remembers the feeling of being constantly under scrutiny.

"I found myself restricted and isolated from my fellow men, followed by officers of the Special Branch wherever I went." Mandela was banned almost continuously for nine years beginning in 1952. As soon as one ban expired, another banning order was issued. In addition to the limits it placed on his political work, the banning had a restrictive effect on his law practice. In 1953, he and Oliver Tambo had set up a law partnership in Johannesburg. Among their clients were many fellow activists who were facing charges from the Defiance Campaign and other protests. Despite the difficulties he faced as a result of being banned, Mandela continued to work at the law office, usually in the evenings.

By the mid-1950s, Mandela had begun to fear that the ANC itself might be banned. He wanted it to stay alive and active if this happened, so he came up with a plan that would change the formal ANC organization, with its body of officials and its membership rolls, into a loosely connected federation of small, secret groups called street cells, in which members' identities would be protected. The ANC leaders approved the plan—which was called the M Plan after Mandela—and agreed to adopt it if necessary.

In 1955, the ANC and half a dozen other groups of political activists agreed to hold a joint meeting to unify the anti-apartheid spirit. The resulting Congress of the People, as it was called, lasted several days and was attended by almost 3,000 delegates from around the country, including 320 Asians, 230 Coloureds, and 112 whites. Many of them wore headcloths, armbands, shirts, or shawls in the ANC colors, green, gold, and black. The delegates voted to accept a document called the Freedom Charter, which outlined proposals for racial equality and democracy in South Africa. Later, activists would collect nearly a million signatures in support of the Charter.

Mandela was under a banning order when the Congress of the People opened the morning of June 26 in Kliptown. To attend would mean breaking the law. But he could not resist the urge to be part of this historic occasion, so he mingled unobtrusively with the crowd, rejoicing in the shouts of *"Afrika!"* and *"Amandla!"* ("power!") that greeted each speaker. He noticed a large number of plainclothes and uniformed police, however, and he began to fear that the Congress might end in disaster. On the afternoon of the second day, his fears proved realistic. An armed battalion of military police burst into the meeting hall and mounted the stage. They announced that no one would be permitted to leave until the names of everyone present had been taken. The building and the square outside were sealed off by police units to prevent any escapes.

The police were kept busy late into the evening questioning each of the thousands of delegates and demanding to see passes and permits. Darkness fell, and lamps were lit in the meeting hall. Someone began singing a slow, sad song. One by one, the rest of the delegates joined in. The police worked on. Finally the interrogations were finished and the delegates were permitted to leave. On December 9, 1956, 156 of them, including Mandela, were arrested on charges of treason because they had attended the Congress.

Ironically, one effect of the arrests was that nearly all of the leaders of the national resistance movement were jailed together in Johannesburg. They got to know one another, held day-long meetings, and made plans for the future. The unity that was fostered among these treason defendants actually strengthened the resistance in the long run.

The pretrial hearing opened with violence. A huge crowd of supporters was waiting in the street to cheer the defendants when they got out of the police vans to enter the courtroom. Frightened by the crowd, the guards began firing and 22 people were hurt. Meanwhile, inside the courtroom, all 156 defendants were locked into a single large cage. Someone had attached a sign to it that said "DON'T FEED," as if the prisoners were animals in a zoo. At this point, the defendants' attorneys successfully demanded that the prisoners be released on bail. As a result, Mandela was able to live at home during the trial.

The Treason Trial started in Pretoria in 1956 and lasted for five agonizing years. During that time, Mandela had to get up early nearly every day to take the bus to Pretoria. After spending the day at the trial and returning to Johannesburg, he devoted the evening hours to his law practice and to ANC duties. It was nearly impossible for him to leave Johannesburg for more than a few hours, because he was required to sign in at the police station every other day. He bitterly resented the way the long-drawn-out trial ate up his time and energy and kept him from the day-to-day activities of the ANC and the resistance movement. And while the trial was going on, his marriage was suffering from stress as well.

He and Evelyn were no longer happy together. They separated in 1956 and received a divorce in 1957. Both of them continued to live in Orlando, their houses a few miles apart. The three children lived with Evelyn but visited Mandela often. Thembi, who was eight years old when the divorce took place, was unhappy about it and grew apart from his father. Makgatho and Makaziwe retained closer ties with Mandela, although the separation was hard on them as well. Evelyn eventually opened a small business of her own, a grocery shop that she called the Mandela Trading Store, in a village called Cofimvaba at the edge of the Transkei. She lives there today.

In 1957, while waiting for his divorce to become final, Mandela met and fell in love with a young social worker from Pondoland, in his native Transkei. Her name was Nomzamo Zanyiwe Winifred Madikizela, and she was called Winnie. She fell deeply in love with Mandela, and before long he had introduced her to his friends and his children. Soon after his divorce was final, in 1958, they planned to marry.

Kokani, Winnie's father, was worried about his daughter's prospects for happiness with a political agitator who was already on trial for treason. She was so determined to marry Mandela, however, that he gave in and granted formal permission. The wedding took place on June 14, 1958, at Winnie's family home in Bizana, in the Transkei. The authorities agreed to relax the ban on Mandela for six days so that he could leave Johannesburg for the ceremony.

The wedding was an elaborate and festive occasion. Winnie wore a white satin gown. Her bridesmaids were two friends and Mandela's sister Leabie. The car in which the bride was driven to church was draped with the green, gold, and black of the ANC. At the church, one minister delivered the marriage service. Another minister, dressed in the animal skins and traditional ornaments of Winnie's tribe, sang the praises of the Madiba and Madikizela clans in the traditional manner. The wedding party drove to the ancestral burying ground of the Madikizelas for feasting, singing, and dancing. In keeping with tradition, Mandela presented a ceremonial headcloth to each of Winnie's female relatives. Later in the day, a great party was held for the newlyweds in the Bizana town hall. In his speech, the bride's father said, "This marriage will be no bed of roses; it is threatened from all sides and only the deepest love will preserve it.'' Fortunately for the high spirits of the celebration, no one knew how true those words would be.

Four days later, Mandela and Winnie returned to Johannesburg. There they settled into family life. Mandela's mother and sister lived with them, and his children were often there as well. In 1959, a daughter was born to Mandela and Winnie. She was given the name Zenani and the nickname Zeni. The following year, Winnie gave birth to a second daughter, Zindziswa, who was called Zindzi.

At the end of the 1950s, Mandela's family life was happy but business and politics were not going well for him. The demands of the Treason Trial and his ANC work meant that there was very little time left for his law practice, which all but disappeared. As a result, the family had to cope with financial problems. The trial dragged on. Finally, in March 1961, Mandela and the others were pronounced not guilty of treason. According to the judge, the government prosecutors had not proved that the ANC or the Congress of the People promoted the violent overthrow of the government. After five years and an appalling waste of time and energy, the trial was over. When the defendants left the courtroom for the last time, they were greeted with cheering and singing in the streets. But for Nelson Mandela, the end of the Treason Trial was only the beginning of a new and dangerous kind of resistance.

Events had taken place in South Africa in 1960 that had shocked the world and convinced Mandela that the time had come to take up arms against apartheid.

# 7

# Sharpeville and the Underground

T HE TRAGEDY OF 1960—a bloody clash between blacks and whites that ended in a
massacre—was rooted in South Africa's long
history of racial hatred. But the politics of the late
1950s contributed to the tragedy.

For one thing, the Nationalist government's
apartheid policies grew ever more oppressive. In
1959, the few legislators who had been allowed to
represent Africans in the parliament—although
the Africans were not permitted to vote for them—
were dismissed. That same year, the government
passed a new education law that further limited
opportunities for African students to attend col-
leges and universities. In the meantime, a split had
occurred within the ranks of the ANC.

In 1958, the extreme pro-Africanist wing of the
movement left the ANC and formed a new organization called the Pan-Africanist Congress (PAC).
Although Mandela liked and respected Robert Sobukwe, the president of the PAC, he felt that the
Africanists were wrong to shrug off the support of

those Asians, Coloureds, and whites who opposed apartheid. He feared that the Africanists would merely substitute black racism for white racism. He also suspected that rivalry between the ANC and the PAC would weaken both organizations and harm the resistance movement.

Matters came to a head in 1960, when both the ANC and the PAC decided to organize mass protests against the hated pass laws. The PAC protest was scheduled for March 21, ten days before the ANC campaign was to begin. On the morning of March 21, Sobukwe and about 150 of his followers marched to the police station in Orlando and announced that they were not carrying their passes. This was a clear violation of the law. They challenged the police to arrest them, and the police obliged.

Similar scenes took place around the country that morning. In the suburbs of Johannesburg, PAC workers guided protesters to the buses that would carry them to the police stations. By midmorning, there were 20,000 protesters in the Johannesburg suburb of Evaton, 4,000 in Vanderbijlpark, which is located between Johannesburg and the nearby white city of Vereeniging, and 2,000 in Cape Town. But it was in Sharpeville, an African township near Vereeniging, that the tension exploded.

About 5,000 protesters jammed the streets, chanting *"Afrika!"* and *"Amandla!"* The government grew desperately afraid that it was losing control of the situation. Police flowed into Sharpeville and air force helicopters buzzed overhead. Then the police opened fire on the crowd. Within moments, 69 of the protesters, including eight women and ten children, were dead. Many of them had been shot in the back as they tried to flee. Another 180 were wounded.

Word of the massacre spread quickly through the black townships and beyond. The Nationalists were strongly criticized in the world press, but they claimed that the shootings had been necessary "to restore order." Mandela, listening in horror to incoming reports of the tragedy, soon learned that two Africans had been killed by police in Cape Town that same day. Within a week, riots in Cape Town would leave 14 more people dead.

Luthuli, president of the ANC, announced that March 28 would be a day of mourning for those slain at Sharpeville. He urged workers to stay home on that day and to burn their passes. The response was overwhelming. Almost all the country's nonwhite workers failed to show up for work. At dusk, Mandela, Luthuli, and other ANC leaders met in Orlando in violation of their banning orders. Watched by hundreds of chanting supporters, they ceremoniously set their passes on fire. Bonfires sprang up around the township and people paraded through the streets, throwing passes into the fires and singing.

Before dawn on March 30, Mandela woke to the sounds of a police raid. He was arrested and taken to jail. The government banned the ANC and the PAC and declared a state of emergency. Oliver Tambo escaped the police dragnet and slipped across the border, traveling illegally without a passport. The ANC had decided that Tambo should head its operations from abroad. He has spent the years since 1960 in England and various black republics in Africa. During the 1980s, he

In March 1960, South African police opened fire on thousands of unarmed people who were demonstrating against apartheid in the city of Sharpeville. Sixty-nine people were killed, and scores wounded. Some of them are shown in this photograph, waiting for medical attention. The Sharpeville massacre was to have a major effect on Nelson Mandela's life.

presided over the ANC from headquarters in Lu-
saka, Zambia.

Not until the state of emergency was lifted in August 1960 was Mandela released from jail. Several
months later, the treason trial ended in acquittal.
By this time, he had had nearly a year to reflect
on the tragedy at Sharpeville. He had come to the
conclusion that the racist policies of the Nationalist government could not be changed through
peaceful, nonviolent means. A government that
could fire into a crowd of unarmed protesters could
not be won over by discussion, argument, or passive resistance. It was time for violent opposition.

Mandela did not come to this conclusion lightly.
The ANC had always claimed to be a nonviolent
organization, a policy which had helped it gain international respectability. But the struggle against
apartheid was growing more desperate by the day.
Mandela decided to go underground—into hiding—to organize an armed opposition movement.

While Mandela was arriving at this decision,
South Africa was facing widespread condemnation from other nations for the Sharpeville massacre and for apartheid. At the same time, the
country's form of government was changing. The
Union of South Africa was a member of the Commonwealth of Nations. This meant that the formal
head of state of the country was Queen Elizabeth II of England, although the actual head of the
government was the South African prime minister. The Nationalists proposed a new constitution
that would change the country to a republic. The
prime minister would still be the effective head of
the government, but the head of state would be a
president. The Nationalists hoped that this change

would loosen the remaining ties between South Africa and Great Britain. It was embarrassing for them when the Queen, who was officially their head of state under the old constitution, openly criticized apartheid.

In 1960, South Africa's white voters agreed to accept the new constitution. In March 1961, the month Mandela's treason trial ended, Prime Minister H. F. Verwoerd of South Africa appeared in London before a meeting of the prime ministers of the Commonwealth countries. He asked them to vote on the question of whether South Africa could remain in the Commonwealth once it became a republic. To his dismay, he was subjected to a torrent of vigorous criticism. The constitutional issue was not under attack. Rather, the criticism was aimed at South Africa's racial policies, most of which had been crafted by Verwoerd himself. It was made clear to Verwoerd that the Commonwealth opposed apartheid in no uncertain terms.

The member nations of the Commonwealth are Great Britain and the countries and territories that were once parts of the British colonial empire. By 1961, however, many of these former colonies were independent nations. Some, such as Canada, New Zealand, and Australia, were mostly white. But others, such as India, Pakistan, Ghana, Nigeria, Kenya, Uganda, and Malawi, gave the Commonwealth a decidedly multiracial quality. When Verwoerd made his request, members of the Commonwealth took the opportunity to point out that apartheid was contrary to the principle of racial equality that the Commonwealth represented. The strongest objections to apartheid came from India, Ghana, and Canada. These nations felt that South

Africa should be expelled from the Commonwealth.

Not all members of the Commonwealth of Nations agreed. In fact, the controversy over apartheid was one of the worst storms that the Commonwealth has had to weather. Some nations felt that it was extremely important to keep this prosperous and productive country, with its many citizens of British descent, in the Commonwealth. Long-standing racial and colonial conflicts among some of the member countries were in danger of being revived. In addition, some of the newly independent member nations with largely black or Asian populations feared that Great Britain would use its prestige and the history of its economic dominance to overshadow their concerns. The very existence of the Commonwealth was threatened. With the Dominion of Canada leading the way, however, the member nations finally agreed to officially condemn apartheid.

In the face of their strong and unanimous protest against racism, Verwoerd withdrew his request for continued membership. South Africa withdrew from the Commonwealth of Nations in May 1961, when the Republic of South Africa was proclaimed. From that time on, South Africa became increasingly isolated from the world community.

The government's plans to change the constitution aroused opposition from the anti-apartheid activists, including Nelson Mandela. Although the ANC and the PAC were banned, their leaders summoned people to a convention in Natal Province at the beginning of May 1961. It was called to protest the establishment of the Republic of South Africa, which was to take effect on May 31. The convention delegates also planned to write a formal demand for democratic government, based on the principle of one person, one vote. About 1,400 delegates appeared.

To their delight, the surprise speaker of the day turned out to be Nelson Mandela, who walked barefoot onto the speaker's platform and electrified them with a firm, lively speech in his distinctive booming voice. His most recent banning order had just expired and this was his first public speech in nine years, other than courtroom speeches during the Treason Trial. The audience applauded him wildly, and Mandela's place as a loved and respected leader was confirmed.

The speakers at the convention, including Mandela, called for strikes by students and workers on May 31, a day for which the Nationalists had planned widespread celebrations in honor of the new republic. Mandela was the leading strike organizer. Since encouraging a strike was against the law, Mandela found himself operating outside the law almost as soon as the Treason Trial ended. While preparing for the May 31 strike, he had to work and travel in secret. He later described himself at this time as "a man who lived the life of an outlaw."

Underground life had little glamour but much danger and inconvenience. He had to use a false name, so he called himself David Motsamai and obtained false identity papers. He was afraid to remain in one place for very long, for fear that informers or police spies would learn of his location. He stayed with friends and supporters. Occasionally he spent a night with friendly strangers.

The government arrested many prominent political activists in the hope of preventing the strike, but it was most eager to arrest Nelson Mandela. Although he had some narrow escapes, a nationwide manhunt failed to catch him. He continued to move swiftly and secretly from place to place, making a brief speech or holding a meeting and then disappearing. Journalists began calling him "the Black Pimpernel," after a famous fictional character called the Scarlet Pimpernel, who possessed a remarkable ability to evade his enemies. From time to time Mandela would stop at a pay telephone and call one of the many reporters who were covering the story of his adventures. His statements to the press were always major news stories.

A few days before the strike, two journalists who had flown in from London to cover the events of May 31 were invited to interview Mandela. They were taken secretly to a house in a white neighborhood where they found him lurking behind drawn curtains. He told them, "The government is spoiling for a massacre. And Africans—well, desperate people will eventually be provoked to acts of retaliation."

The celebrations that had been planned in honor of the new republic fell rather flat. Somewhere between 20 and 50 percent of the nation's workers stayed at home on May 31 because of the strike. The percentage was even higher in Johannesburg, Pretoria, and parts of the Cape Province. The schools had been provided with commemorative flags and medals for the children, but many Asian, African, and Coloured students stayed home or refused to accept the trinkets. School officials had to pack hundreds of thousands of flags and medals back into their boxes and ship them back to Pretoria.

The strike was over, but Mandela remained a fugitive, working on the next phase of the resistance. As a result, he had to endure being separated from Winnie and their two small daughters and from his older children as well. He knew that the police would be watching all the members of his family closely in case he attempted to contact them, so he went for weeks at a time without seeing or speaking to them. The loneliness they all felt was yet another burden imposed by apartheid.

Travel was a problem for Mandela during his underground period. His features were well known around the country from newspaper photographs, so he usually moved from place to place at night, and he became an expert at the art of creating disguises from ordinary objects, such as glasses and caps. He had managed to obtain the use of a car, but it was an old one and often broke down. At one point he disguised himself as a chauffeur so that he could drive around without arousing police curiosity.

Winnie received a tremendous shock one day when she was driving in downtown Johannesburg. A traffic light turned red, and she coasted to a stop next to another car. Glancing casually across, she was stunned to see her husband behind the wheel of the other car with a chauffeur's cap pulled down over his eyes. He stared straight ahead and gave no sign that he had noticed her. She kept her wits and did not call out to him. When the light turned green, the two cars pulled smoothly away from the intersection and they went their separate ways.

Like thousands of other Africans captivated by the saga of the Black Pimpernel, Winnie searched the newspapers each morning to learn where Mandela had last been sighted and what he was doing. On a few occasions, with careful precautions to fool the police, Mandela arranged for Winnie and his children to visit him. Many of these visits took place at a farm called Lilliesleaf, in the Johannesburg suburb of Rivonia. Lilliesleaf was owned by Arthur Goldreich, a white friend who supported the anti-apartheid movement. It was quiet and secluded. Winnie brought Zeni there on several occasions while Mandela was in hiding. Zeni never forgot the place she called "the big house." She remembers her father carrying her through the orchard and taking her for boat rides on the stream that ran through the farm.

To the younger children, Mandela's underground existence at Lilliesleaf seemed almost a game, but his older son Thembi knew how serious it really was. Winnie recalls that even though Thembi was still unhappy over his parents' divorce, he spent a great deal of time with Mandela at Lilliesleaf and other hideouts, helping his father by running errands and carrying messages. Thembi's missions were risky, for he was old enough to be arrested if he were caught. Fortunately, he never was.

Ever since the Defiance of Unjust Laws Campaign of 1952, Africans had celebrated June 26 as Freedom Day. On June 26, 1961, Mandela issued a statement to the press from one of his underground hiding places. In it, he called for renewed, continued opposition to apartheid, and he vowed that he and his fellow ANC members would not give up the fight until South Africa guaranteed equal rights for people of all races. The end of this statement was a resounding pledge of commitment. Mandela said:

> I have had to separate myself from my dear wife and children, from my mother and sisters, to live as an outlaw in my own land. I have had to close my business, to abandon my profession, and live in poverty and misery, as many of my people are doing. . . . I shall fight the government side by side with you, inch by inch, mile by mile, until victory is won. . . . Only through hardship, sacrifice, and militant struggle can freedom be won. The struggle is my life. I will continue fighting for freedom until the end of my days.

Around this time Mandela took the step he had been contemplating for some time and embarked on a program of armed, violent resistance to authority. He organized a small group that called itself Umkhonto we Sizwe (MK), which means "Spear of the Nation." Umkhonto was designed to carry out acts of sabotage against the white government by setting off bombs in government, police, and military buildings. Mandela was named commander in chief, and he wrote a statement in which he announced the intention of the Africans to fight back against apartheid. He also claimed that Umkhonto's purpose was to attack property and buildings only, not to endanger life.

After a few months of planning and training at Lilliesleaf Farm, Umkhonto went into action on

December 16, the anniversary of the battle of Blood River. Bombs exploded in Durban, Johannesburg, and Port Elizabeth. Unfortunately, the saboteurs were clumsy and inexperienced. One was killed and another lost an arm. Umkhonto has remained in existence since 1961 and is recognized as the military branch of the ANC.

Mandela realized immediately after the first explosions that Umkhonto would not be very effective unless it somehow acquired both money and skill. The high-ranking officers of the ANC agreed and decided to send Mandela out of the country to seek support. The independent nations of central, southern, and eastern Africa had scheduled a meeting for early 1962 in Addis Ababa, Ethiopia. The ANC wanted Mandela to represent South Africa there.

Not only was Mandela still wanted by the police for his part in the May strike, but he would be breaking the law again by leaving the country without a passport. The Black Pimpernel was not about to let these minor details stand in his way, however. He was filled with the desire to see something of the world outside South Africa. In particular, he was longing to see how life was lived in the independent black republics elsewhere on the African continent.

On January 11, 1962, Nelson Mandela dressed in a military-style khaki uniform and was driven to the border between South Africa and Bechuanaland (today called Botswana). At a place where there were no border guards, he walked across the frontier.

# 8

# Two Trials

MANDELA'S AFRICAN ODYSSEY began in Bechuanaland, but the South African police were very active there, so his contacts sent him north to Tanganyika (today called Tanzania). He met Julius Nyerere, Tanganyika's leader, and then flew to Lagos, Nigeria, with a companion from the ANC. There he was reunited with Oliver Tambo and with Robert Resha, another friend who had fled South Africa.

New impressions crowded in upon Mandela every day. From his first hour in Bechuanaland, he had been intoxicated by a sense of liberation. He loved being among black Africans who governed themselves proudly and who did not have to live in a constant state of intimidation. He also took delight in discovering the richness and variety of Africa's geography and culture. In Tanganyika, he praised the beauty of the lake-filled landscape. In Nigeria, he was fascinated by the blending of African cultures with Islam, a religion which hardly exists in South Africa. Nigerian clothing, architecture, and even food gave Mandela his first real taste of the Muslim influence.

The next stop was Addis Ababa, where Mandela met Haile Selassie, the emperor of Ethiopia, who promised strong support to the anti-apartheid movement. Then it was time for the conference, and for Mandela's first public appearance since leaving South Africa. He dropped the name David Motsamai and was introduced to the delegates as Nelson Mandela—a name that screamed from the headlines of South Africa's newspapers on the following day. In a long, passionate speech, he summed up the history of oppression and resistance in South Africa. He told his listeners about Sharpeville, about the strikes, bannings, and detentions without trial. He concluded by saying that the freedom movement in South Africa must either fight back or die.

"The government is preparing to strike viciously at political leaders and freedom fighters," he declared, "but the people will not take these blows sitting down." Mandela's call to arms received much applause, and when he left the conference he felt that he had won considerable support for Umkhonto among his African brethren.

Mandela, Tambo, and the others next flew to Cairo, Egypt. Like any tourists, they gazed in awe at the Pyramids and the Sphinx, at the mummies of ancient pharaohs, and the treasures of King Tutankhamen. Then they visited Libya, Tunisia, Morocco, Algeria, Mali, Guinea, Sierra Leone, Liberia, Ghana, and Senegal. Mandela obtained a complete set of each country's traditional women's dress to take home for Winnie.

In each country, he met with as many top officials as possible and tried to obtain either donations of money for Umkhonto or promises of further support. He got help of a different sort in Algeria, where he received instruction in guerrilla warfare techniques from men who were fighting in the Algerian revolution against French colonial control. Mandela took careful notes on these lectures, as he had done when he received some military training in Ethiopia.

One goal of Mandela's mission abroad was to arrange for Umkhonto recruits to be smuggled out of South Africa for military and guerrilla training in other countries. He was successful and the first batch of recruits left South Africa to begin their training in Tanganyika before Mandela returned to his own country in July 1962.

The final leg of the trip took Mandela and Tambo to England. Dawn broke as their plane descended over London, and Mandela looked out his window to see the metropolis sprawling away in all directions below him. Its smoggy haze was shot through by the rays of the rising sun. His first thought was that this was the center of the empire that had invaded and colonized half the world, including his own land. Yet after a few days in London he found himself unable to hold much of a grudge against the city or the British people. He was warmly received by a number of British political leaders and by fellow South Africans who were living in England.

It was July, and Mandela had been away from South Africa for half a year. He knew that he faced tremendous risks if he went home. He was still a fugitive. The South African government, embarrassed and angry that he had escaped their manhunt to make public speeches in other countries, was more eager than ever to catch him. He was not just facing a jail sentence. Acts of sabotage by Umkhonto meant he could be executed. He knew that he could stay safely in England or in one of the African republics, working for the ANC and for Umkhonto from exile as Tambo was doing. Yet his home and his family were in South Africa.

Even more important was direct involvement in the ongoing struggle against apartheid. He felt that his leadership was most needed at home, where he could plan and encourage others by the example of his own actions. Taking his life in his hands, he returned.

He slipped across the border into South Africa at an unchecked, prearranged spot and was met by one of the Umkhonto commanders in a car. He was taken to Lilliesleaf Farm, where he plunged back into the underground life of a fugitive. The South African authorities heard many rumors that the Black Pimpernel had returned and was in the Johannesburg area. By now they were utterly determined to capture him. He had incited a strike, he had left the country illegally, and most galling of all to the police, he had eluded capture for more than a year, flaunting his liberty all across Africa as well as in England.

In early August, Mandela decided to go to Durban to meet with Chief Luthuli and other banned ANC leaders. He disguised himself in the chauffeur's outfit and drove the car of Cecil Williams, a white friend who pretended to be his boss. On August 5, after his meeting with Luthuli, Mandela went to a party attended by ANC members and sympathizers. The group joked about the fact that the police were searching high and low for Mandela. Someone said, "Wouldn't they love to know that he's right here under their noses?" and everyone laughed.

Later that day Mandela and his "boss" got into the car and drove out of Durban, headed for Rivonia. Williams was driving. They had been traveling for an hour and a half when Williams glanced into the rearview mirror.

"Nelson," he said urgently. "There's a police car on our tail." A moment later, the police car, traveling at top speed, had caught up with them.

Mandela considered his chances. One side of the road was a high embankment. He thought that if he could only dash across the road and clamber up the bank, he might be able to lose himself in the countryside. He had to decide at once. He glanced behind the car again and saw that the first police car had been joined by two more. His heart sank. There was no chance to make a break for it. He would be shot down the moment he left the car.

The police cars forced Williams to a stop at the side of the road. Mandela was carrying a gun and a diary. Matters would be far worse for him if he was caught with an illegal weapon, and he was afraid that his diary would give the authorities damaging evidence against his friends and supporters. He searched frantically for a hiding place and found a crevice in the car's upholstery between the two front seats. He shoved the gun and the diary in as far as possible. Almost the next second a police sergeant loomed at the passenger window and asked to see Mandela's pass.

Mandela handed over his false identity papers.

The sergeant replied, "I know you are Nelson Mandela. I have here a warrant for your arrest." The daring escapes of the Black Pimpernel were over.

Later, it was rumored that the police had been tipped off to Mandela's location by the host of the party in Durban. Winnie learned of the arrest the next day when she read the newspaper headlines: "Police Swoop Ends Two Years On The Run" and "Nelson Mandela Under Arrest".

Mandela's trial took place in Pretoria in October and November 1962. He faced two charges: encouraging a strike and leaving the country without a passport. On the first day of the trial, he entered the courtroom looking regal in a leopard-skin kaross, which is a Thembu cloak worn over one shoulder. Winnie appeared in a long dress covered with beads, the traditional dress of Thembu royalty. This dramatic gesture of African pride drew cheers from the spectators, and the irritated judge ordered Winnie not to wear her tribal garb again. Throughout the rest of the trial, however, many of the African women among the spectators wore tribal clothing. Winnie dressed in the outfits that Mandela had brought her from other African nations.

The state presented its case against Nelson Mandela. On November 7, 1962, acting as his own defense attorney, Mandela delivered an hour-long statement to the packed courtroom. In it, he admitted that he had encouraged the strike and left the country illegally, but he tried to make the court understand why. It was here that he spoke of his boyhood spent listening to the tales of Tatu Joyi and the dream of restoring self-government to the African people. He spoke about the ANC and its

89

fifty-year history of attempts to negotiate with the white government. And he explained why, as a citizen, as a black man, and as a person of conscience he had found himself unable to obey laws that were "unjust, immoral, and intolerable" because they were based on racial discrimination.

Ten minutes after Mandela's speech ended, he was pronounced guilty and sentenced to five years in prison. In May 1963, after six months in jail in Pretoria, came the harrowing transfer in the closed van to dreaded Robben Island.

At the island, Mandela worked on a labor crew that was assigned to pound boulders into gravel. He was banned while in prison, so that it was illegal for anyone to quote him or to publish his words. He was not permitted to receive mail and Winnie was not allowed to visit him until July. At that time, she made the 900-mile journey from Johannesburg to Cape Town and was permitted to spend 30 minutes talking with Mandela in a crude, wooden shack at the edge of the island, with warders present to hear every word. The couple was ordered to speak English or Afrikaans so that the guards would understand.

"I was so depressed when I came away," says Winnie of this visit. "But at least I had seen Nelson and he had appeared pleased and relieved to see me."

A few months later, Mandela was suddenly told that he was being sent back to Pretoria to stand trial on a new charge. This time he was accused of sabotage and trying to overthrow the government by violent revolution. Under South African law, he could receive the death penalty.

The new trial resulted from a police action

against Umkhonto we Sizwe. Government authorities had managed to place several informers inside Umkhonto, and one of these informers discovered that Lilliesleaf Farm was the underground headquarters of the Umkhonto high command. Late at night on July 11, 1963, a bakery truck and a dry cleaner's delivery van drove into Rivonia and pulled into the driveway of Lilliesleaf. Armed police with attack dogs crept from the vans and melted into the darkness, surrounding the house and outbuildings. A police officer threw open a door and the sixteen people inside the room leaped up in shock. One man tried to escape through a window, only to be driven back by a snarling police dog. That man was Walter Sisulu. He and the others were charged with sabotage and attempting to overthrow the state. Mandela, as head of Umkhonto's high command, was also accused.

The Rivonia Trial, as it came to be called, opened on October 9, 1963, in Pretoria. Winnie was permitted to attend the trial, but again was warned not to appear in tribal attire. At each session she appeared in everyday clothing—in the defiant ANC colors of green, gold, and black. Mandela's mother, Nosekeni Fanny Mandela, made her way from the Transkei to attend.

For five months, the government presented its case against the prisoners, who were charged with a total of 199 acts of sabotage. The state claimed that the ANC had started its program of sabotage in late 1961 in order to pave the way for a violent revolution in which the Africans would overthrow the government entirely and turn South Africa into a Communist state. The notes Mandela had taken during his guerrilla training in Algeria were introduced by the government's lawyers as evidence that Mandela was planning a military takeover.

In April 1964, the defense attorneys began to present their case. They argued several points: that the ANC was not controlled by the Communist Party (although they admitted that the ANC and the CP were closely linked and shared many ideals and goals); that Umkhonto we Sizwe had been formed to carry out strategic sabotage rather than open revolution; and that the court should take into consideration the pressing moral reasons why Mandela and the others believed they had to take action against apartheid.

The case for the defense began with a statement from Mandela, explaining his background and the formation of Umkhonto. He said that he had turned to violent resistance only after, in his opinion, all attempts at nonviolent change had failed.

"I did not plan the sabotage in a spirit of recklessness, nor because I have any love for violence," he said. "We believed that as a result of government policy, violence by the African people had become inevitable." He added that, although Umkhonto was to perform sabotage, its members swore not to injure or kill anyone. And he declared proudly, "I have always regarded myself, in the first place, as an African patriot." He concluded, "I have cherished the ideal of a democratic and free society in which all persons live together in harmony with equal opportunities. It is an ideal which I hope to live for and to see realized. But if needs be, it is an ideal for which I am prepared to die." With this last sentence, he acknowledged the fear that all of the Rivonia defendants felt: They

Nelson Mandela outside the courthouse during the Rivonia trial in 1964. Although he could have been condemned to death for treason, because of international pressure the judge sentenced him to life imprisonment. It would be more than two decades before Mandela was freed from prison.

could be hanged for political crimes. Hundreds of activists already had been. There was no reason to think that they would not be next.

The defense case occupied all of May and early June. Throughout the trial, the government in Pretoria received hundreds of protests and petitions urging merciful treatment of the Rivonia defendants. Church groups, human rights organizations, and individuals from all over the world wrote to plead that the death penalty not be applied. Criticism of the trial from the governments of other nations, especially from India and the African republics, also put pressure on the Nationalists. South Africa's government authorities were aware that the world was closely watching the Palace of Justice in Pretoria. An outcry would arise in the international press if the defendants were executed.

The verdict was delivered on June 11 at the Palace of Justice. All but one of the defendants were found guilty. Outside the building, a priest led a crowd of Africans in prayer. When Winnie appeared on the steps, her head held high despite her grief and fear, the crowd burst into the popular African religious anthem "Nkosi Sikelele" (God bless Africa), which had been adopted as one of the "freedom songs" of the ANC and the anti-apartheid movement in general. It begins:

*God bless Africa.*
*Raise up her name.*
*Hear our prayers and bless us.*
*Come down, Holy Spirit, and bless us,*
*The family of Africa.*

The sentencing took place one day later, on June 12. The packed courtroom waited in tense silence for the magistrate, Mr. Justice de Wet, to pass sentence. De Wet spoke in a dry, measured voice: "The sentence is life imprisonment on all counts for the accused." A wave of relief—mingled with agonizing sadness at the thought of life spent behind bars—ran through the defendants and their families. Tears came to Winnie's eyes, but she did not cry. Outside the Palace of Justice, the whisper of "life—they got life" rippled through the waiting crowd. Everyone felt that the international pressure against the death penalty had saved the lives of Mandela and the other defendants.

The prisoners were marched from the courtroom into a police van. Their families and supporters strained to catch a glimpse of them. Mandela was able to wave to Winnie as he was led into the van. Prisoners and spectators joined in a single great cry of *"Amandla!"* Then the van drove away. That night the prisoners were flown to Cape Town and once again, ferried across the harbor to the forbidding prison on Robben Island.

# 9

# The World's Most Famous Prisoner

MANDELA FACED THE prospect of spending the rest of his life on Robben Island. He was kept from total despair by the fact that Sisulu and his other comrades from the Rivonia Trial were also there. He knew that they would help and support each other as much as possible. Indeed, so many activists were sent to Robben Island in the mid-1960s after the Rivonia Trial and other treason and sabotage trials, that the government had to build four new barracks to house the political prisoners. Over time, Mandela and the other "politicals," as they were called, established a society of their own within the walls of the prison. They engaged in spirited debates and discussions, sharing ideas and knowledge. Their bodies were imprisoned, but they fought to keep their minds and souls free.

Prison conditions were horrible at first. The food was of poor quality and the African prisoners received even worse food than did prisoners of other races. The cells were unfurnished and the prisoners were given only cold water for washing. As bad as the physical discomforts were, the feeling of being isolated from the rest of the world was worse. The prisoners were supposed to receive no news from the outside. They learned about world events in bits and pieces, however, mostly from hurried conversations with new prisoners or from newspapers that were carelessly left lying about by the warders. Mandela suspects that a few of the warders were somewhat sympathetic to the prisoners and deliberately left papers for them whenever there was a big news story.

Mandela and the other politicals had been condemned to hard labor, which meant that they were roused at five or six each morning, fed, and then marched or driven to a work site on the island. Sometimes they were set to gathering seaweed along the shore. At other times they built or repaired roads. Most of the time, however, they worked in the lime quarry, chipping limestone out of the island's bedrock and then pulverizing the large chunks of stone into gravel or powder with shovels. Mandela describes the quarry work this way: "You begin the task briskly, full of zest, song, and swing, but soon the hard rock takes it all away. The lime is soft, but it is embedded in almost impregnable layers of very hard rock. You strike and it remains implacable. Then the singing changes to swearing and there are altercations with the warders." The limestone dust was the worst part of the job. It was white and fine and hung in a cloud around the quarry, choking the men and stinging their eyes.

Each man adjusted in his own way to prison life. Neville Alexander, an activist who was a prisoner on Robben Island at the same time as Mandela, says that what he missed most was children and the sound of their voices. Ahmed Kathrada, a member of Umkhonto and one of the Rivonia defendants, recalls how desperately he devoured all news of home that arrived in the few letters that prisoners were permitted to receive. He longed for bits of everyday life, such as gossip and picnics and flowers. Jeff Masemola, a PAC activist, gave lessons in mathematics to Mandela and others.

"The worst part of imprisonment is being locked up by yourself," Mandela says. During his own hours and days of isolation, doubts set in. He found himself wondering about his friends and family members on the outside. Were they still loyal to him? Had his sacrifice been worth anything? What might he be doing if he had not gotten involved in politics?

To save themselves from gnawing doubts and worries like these, the prisoners struggled to build a sense of community. People who had been at odds on the outside—rival ANC and PAC members, for example—set their differences aside now that they shared a common fate. The politicals set up committees for discipline, education, recreation, and political and literary discussion. In this community-within-a-prison, Sisulu and Mandela were recognized as leaders, men to whom the other prisoners could turn when they needed to talk to someone, men who worked to protect the prisoners' dignity and rights.

One of the most painful aspects of life in prison was the separation from loved ones. Contact with the outside was strictly limited. Prisoners' letters were censored by the authorities, who cut out anything about politics or political associates. Sometimes letters never reached the prisoners at all. The prisoners were allowed only two each month and two visits each year. Many of their family members were so poor that they could not afford the expense of traveling to Cape Town, even on these rare occasions.

A few months after Mandela was returned to the island, Winnie received permission to visit him. At the same time, her friend Albertina Sisulu received permission to visit her husband. The two women were forbidden to travel together, however, because both of them were under banning orders. Winnie's next visit did not take place until 1966. She visited Mandela again in 1968, and again in 1970. She was able to visit him a few more times during the 1970s and 1980s, and she received help from unexpected sources. In 1982, for example, a woman in England sent Winnie money to pay her airfare from Johannesburg to Cape Town and back. Some international aid organizations provided Winnie and other wives of the political prisoners with funds for the same purpose.

Nelson Mandela suffered greatly by being isolated from his family at times of grief and mourning. In September 1968, his mother died of a heart attack, and he was refused permission to leave prison to attend her funeral in Thembuland. Not quite a year later, he received even more shattering news. His son Thembi had died in an automobile accident. Mandela had been out of touch with Thembi for some years, and his sorrow at his son's death was all the greater because the chance of patching up their relationship was gone. He wrote to Evelyn, expressing his grief and sympathy. It was his first contact with her since their divorce.

Mandela missed sharing his family's joy as well as its grief. He treasured accounts of such family occasions as the school graduations and weddings of his children and the births of his thirteen grandchildren. Letters, cards, and photographs became extremely important to him. He regarded them as lifelines to his family. "As long as I don't hear from you, I will remain worried and dry like a desert," he wrote to Winnie in 1976. "Letters from you and the family are like the arrival of summer rains and springs that liven my life and make it enjoyable."

Three years later, he wrote to her, "Had it not been for your visits, wonderful letters, and your love, I would have fallen apart many years ago. I pause here and drink some coffee, after which I dust the photos on my bookcase."

One of the most difficult burdens Mandela had to bear was the frustration he felt when family members were in trouble and he was powerless to help them. He was deeply disturbed when his son Makgatho left school without graduating, and in many letters he urged the boy to finish his education. He agonized about his inability to be present to guide Makgatho in person. He suffered also through his daughter Maki's divorce, but he rejoiced when she remarried, completed her education, and moved with her new husband to the United States. Zeni and Zindzi, his and Winnie's daughters, were only five and three years old when Mandela was imprisoned before the Rivonia Trial. During his years in prison, they went to school, experienced all the trials and tribulations of adolescence, and started families of their own. He ached to share their lives, but he had to make do with visits, letters, and pictures. These things helped to ease his loneliness, but were never enough to end it.

Worst of all was the separation from Winnie. Not only did he miss her as any devoted husband would miss his wife, but he also worried constantly about the many troubles she endured. During the first two decades of his imprisonment, she was almost constantly under banning orders. Police raids on her home in Orlando and arrests occurred so often that she kept a small suitcase packed by her front door so that she could grab it as she was being hustled off to jail. She was jailed on several occasions. Sometimes she was charged with violating her banning orders, and on other occasions she was simply held for long periods without charges, as South African law permitted. In 1969, she spent five months in solitary confinement. Later she was banished by government order to a dilapidated house in the small town of Brandfort, in the Orange Free State. She was forced to live there for five years before returning to Orlando.

Because of her banning and jailings, she found it difficult to keep a job, and she often had to get by on a frighteningly small income. Mandela's powerlessness to help her was a source of anguish, but the strength and determination Winnie showed in surviving her troubles became a source of pride to him.

If the South African government had hoped to silence the voices that were crying out against apartheid by imprisoning the Rivonia defendants and banning their wives, its strategy backfired.

Over the years of Mandela's imprisonment, his stature increased, as did Winnie's, both in South Africa and around the world. Mandela came to be recognized as a symbol of resistance against racial oppression. Messages from him were carried out into the world by prisoners who were released from Robben Island, and the writings that Mandela managed to smuggle out of prison from time to time made him a spokesperson for freedom and human rights at home and abroad.

As the 1960s and 1970s passed, Mandela became a legend. Although he was confined to a prison cell, his spirit was alive in the worldwide anti-apartheid movement. From the beginning of his imprisonment, he received honors and awards from a variety of organizations around the world. These awards from student groups, churches, human rights organizations, and the like did nothing to change his actual situation, of course, but they showed him—and the South African government—how highly he was regarded in many countries. In 1964, for example, the students at University College in London elected Mandela the honorary president of their students' union. The following year, students at the University of Leeds, also in England, did the same thing. A nuclear particle discovered by scientists at the University of Leeds in 1973 was named the Mandela particle in his honor. In 1979, India gave its highest civic award, the Nehru Award for International Understanding, to Mandela, and he was made an honorary doctor of law by the University of Lesotho.

The worldwide admiration of Mandela did not go unnoticed by the South African authorities. His stature as a hero of the struggle against racism helped change the treatment of political prisoners starting in the 1970s. Petitions from the prisoners to the governor of the prison and to authorities outside the island also helped. Cells were eventually equipped with benches and bookshelves, and later with writing tables and chairs. Hot water was piped in to the showers. Prisoners were allowed to take correspondence courses from high schools and universities on the mainland. Mandela took a number of courses in economics and law by mail from London University. By the mid-1970s, prisoners were allowed to subscribe to a handful of magazines that were on the prison authorities' "approved" list. There was also a small prison library, although the quality of the books was a constant source of distress—the prisoners wanted texts on geography, history, economics, and political science, but most of the books were popular novels.

There was a small courtyard where the prisoners could play volleyball or tennis during their recreation breaks, and they were provided with cards, chessboards, and other indoor games. A movie was shown once a month. The prisoners, of course, had no say in the selection of the film. Eventually, the prisoners were permitted to receive newspapers, to listen to the radio, and finally even to watch television.

Improvements in the quality of prison life were a good thing, said Mandela's supporters, but freedom would be even better. They called upon the South African government to release him and the other Rivonia defendants. In 1973, the government *did* offer to set Mandela free, but under certain conditions. He would be released from prison *only* if he agreed to live in the Bantustan of the Transkei and to remain there permanently, under the supervision of the Bantustan authorities and their superiors in the central government. Such an agreement would have meant that Mandela could not participate in political activity. His power to inspire others would be severely limited if he were confined to a Bantustan. In addition, he hated the Bantustan system because it was merely a way of keeping the African people from winning a place within the larger government. It is said that he was offered his freedom as many as five times on the condition that he settle quietly in the Transkei. He refused each time.

In the years after the Rivonia Trial, the white leaders of South Africa took strong action against the organizations and individuals that opposed their rule. They banned the ANC and the PAC. They also banned many people who spoke out against apartheid, including a number of white liberal thinkers and activists. Dozens of political activists were tried and sentenced to imprisonment. Some were executed. By silencing the spokesmen and spokeswomen of the anti-apartheid movement, the government hoped to bring the movement to a halt.

In 1966, Verwoerd was succeeded as prime minister by B. J. Vorster, who headed the most extreme part of the Nationalist Party. Vorster was deeply committed to protecting the apartheid system and to keeping South Africa a white man's country. Under his leadership, repression of the African, Asian, and Coloured populations was greater than ever. Even trivial apartheid regulations were enforced with renewed strictness.

But strong pressure can create stronger resistance and that is what happened in South Africa. Resistance to apartheid not only continued but gained strength with the passing years. While the imprisoned Nelson Mandela was gaining worldwide recognition as a symbol of resistance to racial oppression, the struggle in South Africa was taking on new forms, with new leaders.

In the early 1970s, a new generation of young people came of age in South Africa. Inspired by the example of Mandela, Sisulu, and their comrades, these young people formed new organizations to fight against apartheid. One of the most important of these was called Black Consciousness (BC). It arose among university students and religious groups. Its center was the black medical school at the University of Natal, and its leader was an African student named Steve Biko.

Black Consciousness was influenced by the black power movement in the United States. It emphasized pride and independence as the principal qualities Africans should cultivate. Biko and other BC spokespeople felt that South Africa's blacks needed to work for liberation on their own, that they could no longer depend on the efforts of white liberals in South Africa and abroad, who meant well but were not very effective. Another important youth group was the South African Students Organization (SASO). Women also became more involved in political activism through such groups as the Soweto Parents Association and the Black Women's Federation. Winnie Mandela belonged to both of these organizations.

By the mid-1970s, South Africa was a simmering kettle of anger and bitterness ready to boil over. The boiling point was reached in June 1976. The government had recently enacted a law that required black schools to use Afrikaans, the Dutch-based language of the ruling white Afrikaner class, rather than English, Zulu, Sotho, or Xhosa. Classes were to be taught and examinations were to be taken in Afrikaans. But most African students knew little or no Afrikaans. In fact, a great many of their teachers could not read or write it. It quickly became clear that huge numbers of African students would not pass the all-important matriculation examinations because of this newly imposed language barrier. Spontaneous demonstrations against Afrikaans broke out in black townships all over South Africa.

The largest demonstration took place in Soweto, the huge black township near Johannesburg that includes the Mandelas' Orlando neighborhood. On June 16, 10,000 angry students took to the streets with banners and posters to protest the language law. They marched toward one of the African schools, where the police tried to turn them back with tear gas and dogs. When the oncoming students refused to turn back, the police began firing into the crowd, killing a number of children. The crowd went wild and the protest became a riot—the worst in South Africa's history. African children and teenagers ran through the streets, hurling stones, overturning cars and buses, and setting fire to scores of buildings. By the day's end, a pall of smoke hung over Soweto. After dark it was illuminated by the glow of hundreds of fires.

The rioting spread to other African communities, which rose up in outrage not just against the new language law but against the entire system of apartheid. By the time the police restored order several weeks later, more than 600 people had been killed and more than 1,500 were injured. Thousands of homes had been burned.

From his prison cell, Mandela summed up the tragedy of the Soweto uprisings when he said, "The verdict of June 16 is clear: Apartheid has failed."

# 10

# Winds of Change

LIKE SHARPEVILLE IN 1960, the Soweto riots of 1976 marked a turning point in South African history. Black leaders, many of whom were young people, were more fiercely determined than ever to keep fighting. Just as Umkhonto we Sizwe had been born out of Mandela's rage and desperation following Sharpeville, a handful of new underground guerrilla organizations were born after Soweto. At the same time, many new recruits joined Umkhonto and some of them were secretly sent out of the country for military training in Angola, Zambia, and other black republics.

Not all of the new African organizations were dedicated to violent resistance. A group called Inkatha was founded by Mangosuthu Gatsha Buthelezi, chief of the large Zulu tribe. Today Inkatha has 1.5 million members and is still headed by Buthelezi. He supports nonviolent change, and Inkatha is usually regarded as more conservative—

that is, somewhat less hostile to the existing government—than the ANC. Inkatha rejected the ANC's close ties with communism. But Inkatha was only one of many new movements, and most were dedicated to an armed struggle against apartheid.

Acts of sabotage and shootouts between blacks and whites occurred increasingly often. More and more of these defiant measures were aimed at people, rather than at property. Bombs in white shopping centers and sports arenas took dozens of lives. The authorities reacted with bannings, beatings, and arrests.

Steve Biko of the Black Consciousness movement was one of those arrested. He died in September 1977 at age 30, while being questioned by police. His death immediately brought a renewed outcry against apartheid and police brutality. Both inside South Africa and in the world press, the South African government faced a storm of criticism that grew harsher all the time.

Criticism was nothing new to the Nationalists. Almost since the day they came to power in 1948 other countries had voiced their disapproval of apartheid at the United Nations, at meetings of the Commonwealth of Nations, and elsewhere. As early as 1948, the United Nations General Assembly had condemned South Africa's racial policies. The United Nations Security Council formally criticized apartheid in 1960. However, a movement within the United Nations in the mid-1960s to put South Africa under economic sanctions—that is, to forbid member countries from engaging in trade with or investment in South Africa—failed. Powerful Western nations, including the United States, Great Britain, and France, refused to agree to sanctions.

Americans wrestled for years with the question of sanctions. The issue weighed ethical values against military security and economic interests. On the one hand, nearly everyone agreed that apartheid was morally wrong. But on the other, many political leaders were reluctant to make an enemy of the South African government, especially in the 1960s. These were the years of what is called the Cold War—a period of tremendous tension and hostility between communist and noncommunist nations, with widespread fear that another world war could break out. Because of its location on the seaway between the Atlantic and Indian oceans, South Africa would have great strategic importance in the event of such a war, and the Western powers did not want to lose what might be their only ally in Africa.

In addition, the mines of South Africa were a major source of mineral supplies to the noncommunist world. The United States alone imports two thirds of its platinum, half of its chromium, and one third of its manganese from South Africa. By the late 1970s, however, the Cold War had waned and many people in the West called upon their governments to use economic pressure to force South Africa to ease apartheid. Although the United States and Great Britain held off on sanctions, a number of European countries did enact them, limiting or eliminating trade with South Africa and preventing their businesses from building factories there.

South Africa began to become something of an

outcast in the world community. Its white athletes were barred from the Olympic Games and some other international sports events. Its racism was publicly condemned in scores of nations by everyone from schoolchildren to presidents, church leaders to movie stars.

Events in southern Africa in the late 1970s deepened South Africa's isolation. The neighboring states of Angola, Mozambique, and Southern Rhodesia had been ruled, like South Africa, by white minorities. Between 1975 and 1980, the black majorities won control of these nations. Southern Rhodesia's name was changed to Zimbabwe. This left South Africa alone as the only white-ruled regime on the continent.

Increasingly, the Nationalist Party felt itself besieged on all sides. And just as the black regimes, such as Tanganyika's, were helping the ANC, Umkhonto, and other guerrilla and anti-apartheid groups, the South African government lent financial and military aid to the embattled whites of other African countries, sometimes boldly sending troops of the South African Defense Force (SADF) across the border into Mozambique or Angola to attack black guerrilla forces or, later, the black governments. By doing so, the Nationalists hoped that they would be able to threaten government stability in these emerging black republics, preventing them in turn from encouraging or aiding the anti-apartheid movement in South Africa.

Battles continued at home as well as beyond South Africa's borders. In 1980, people in Soweto rioted to protest rent increases and the police and army were sent into the township to restore order. Bombings increased. Twenty people were killed and almost 200 injured when a black activist group exploded a car bomb in Pretoria in 1983. One of the bloodiest incidents took place in 1988, when a bomb exploded at a white rugby stadium, killing dozens and injuring hundreds. As the decade wore on, violence among black activist groups became increasingly common. Just as the rivalry between the ANC and the PAC had threatened black solidarity in the 1950s, rivalries between the ANC and Inkatha, and among other splinter groups and factions now threatened the entire anti-apartheid movement. Mandela followed these developments from prison, and they worried him deeply.

But the 1980s also brought new developments in Mandela's life. In April 1982, he was transferred from Robben Island to Pollsmoor, a prison on the mainland near Cape Town. Walter Sisulu, Ahmed Kathrada, and two other political prisoners were sent to Pollsmoor from the Island at the same time. The five men shared a single large cell with another Pollsmoor prisoner. Mandela, however, remained foremost in the public mind. The flow of international recognition that had begun in the 1970s became a flood in the 1980s. He received honorary degrees from universities in Belgium, the United States, and England, and in 1985 the London Council erected a bronze statue of Mandela that was captioned "The Struggle Is My Life." Zeni Mandela and Oliver Tambo came to London for the ceremony to unveil the statue. They told the assembled crowds that they hoped that Zeni's father would soon be able to see the statue for himself.

Worldwide recognition of Mandela was not limited to formal organizations. Streets and parks in many countries bear his name today because people in those communities—often students and young people—wrote petitions and held rallies. Students in a number of schools organized "Nelson Mandela Days," during which they read his speeches aloud and collected signatures for petitions to the South African government on his behalf. In 1984, the British rock group Special AKA released a record called "Free Nelson Mandela." It became a hit and was played on radio stations around the world, helping to make Mandela a popular hero to a new generation. From Cairo to Cleveland, teenagers started wearing T-shirts and buttons that bore Mandela's picture or slogans calling for his release. That same year, Bishop Desmond Tutu was awarded the Nobel Peace Prize. He is a black cleric of the Anglican Church in South Africa (today he is Archbishop of Cape Town). Over the years, he had repeatedly called the world's attention to the cruelties of apartheid and had urged the government to release Mandela.

The demand for Mandela's release echoed again and again during the 1980s. In 1981, the South African embassy in France received a petition signed by 17,000 people that urged the South African government to release Mandela and other political prisoners. In early 1982, a similar petition began circulating among the mayors of European cities. By August more than 2,000 mayors of cities in 53 countries around the world had signed it. That same year, the Organization of African Unity, an association of independent black states, publicly called upon South Africa to release Mandela.

In 1983, 78 members of the British parliament signed a petition calling for his release. The Dutch parliament voted to request the freedom of all political prisoners in South Africa, and as a result the Netherlands government notified South Africa that it was willing to give political asylum—that is, grant permanent residence and haven in the Netherlands—to Nelson and Winnie Mandela.

In 1984, a bill sponsored by 135 congressmen in the United States House of Representatives called for Mandela's release. It was passed in the House and also in the Senate. Also in 1984, the secretary general of the United Nations received a petition signed by 50,000 people around the world pleading with the South African government to set Mandela free. In 1985, the Reverend Allan Boesak, an anti-apartheid activist and head of the World Alliance of Reformed Churches, led a march on Pollsmoor to call for Mandela's freedom. He was arrested and spent a month in jail.

It so happened that Mandela *had* been offered his freedom in January 1985. P. W. Botha, who was then the prime minister, wrote to Mandela and the other Rivonia defendants telling them that they would be released if they would give up their membership in the ANC—which was still officially banned in South Africa—and renounce, or give up, the policy of "violent struggle" against apartheid. In other words, they could go free if they urged the African people to refrain from strikes and all forms of armed resistance to apartheid. The defendants rejected the conditions of this offer. Mandela was assigned to write the statement of rejection.

His statement was read to a crowd of 10,000

supporters at a stadium in Soweto on February 10, 1985, by his daughter Zindzi. In it, Mandela declared proudly: "I am a member of the African National Congress. I have always been a member of the African National Congress and I will remain a member of the African National Congress until I die." Then he asked the assembled listeners, "What freedom am I being offered while the organization of the people remains banned? What freedom am I being offered when I may be arrested on a pass offense? What freedom am I being offered to live my life as a family with my dear wife, who remains in banishment at Brandfort? What freedom am I being offered when I must ask for permission to live in an urban area? What freedom am I being offered when I need a stamp in my pass to seek work? What freedom am I being offered when my very South African citizenship is not respected?"

He concluded by saying, "Only free men can negotiate. Prisoners cannot enter into contracts. . . . I cannot and will not give any undertaking at a time when I and you, the people, are not free. Your freedom and mine cannot be separated." The closing words of the statement were, "I will return."

United States president Ronald Reagan, a conservative, was opposed to sanctions against South Africa, but by the mid-1980s the Reagan administration could no longer resist public demand. In 1985, the United States enacted moderate sanctions that curbed some trade. Among other things, the sanctions made it illegal for Americans to buy Krugerrands, the gold coins of South Africa. In 1986, stricter sanctions were passed by the United

States government. Pressure from stockholders and customers also caused many American corporations to voluntarily stop investing in South Africa as a protest against apartheid. But still Mandela remained in prison, and Botha's government showed no sign of softening.

July 1988 brought Mandela's seventieth birthday. Celebrations in his honor were held all over the world. Dignitaries, such as Pope John Paul II and French president François Mitterand, announced birthday greetings to Mandela and renewed their calls for his release. Birthday gifts and cards poured into South Africa from all over. The people of the Netherlands alone sent more than 170,000 of them. One unusual gift came from the boxer Mike Tyson. He sent Mandela the boxing gloves with which he had won the world heavyweight championship.

Of all the birthday celebrations, none was more spectacular then Freedomfest, an 11-hour rock concert in London dedicated to Mandela and the end of apartheid. Freedomfest was sponsored by Artists Against Apartheid. It had a television audience of more than one billion people in more than 60 countries—the largest audience for a music event in the history of television. More than 72,000 people attended in person. Oliver Tambo of the ANC and other activists sat in the special seats that are usually reserved for members of Britain's royal family. They saw and heard such stars as Whitney Houston, George Michael, the Eurhythmics, Stevie Wonder, Tracy Chapman, Natalie Cole, Phil Collins, the Bee Gees, Steve Van Zandt (who sang his anti-apartheid song "Sun City"), and Eric Clapton.

Sting sang his hit "If You Love Somebody Set Them Free." The group Dire Straits, which has been banned in South Africa since 1979 for donating money to the human rights organization Amnesty International, dedicated "Brothers in Arms" to Mandela. Harry Belafonte opened the concert by saluting Mandela and saying, "We want to see you and your fellow prisoners free." American opera singer Jessye Norman closed it with the song "Amazing Grace." As she sang, fireworks over London's skyline saluted the absent guest of honor, who was in a maximum security prison cell at the other end of the earth.

Just a few weeks after his birthday, Mandela fell ill and was taken to the police ward of a Cape Town hospital, where Winnie and Zindzi flew at once to see him. He had lost weight and looked old and tired. He had been stricken with tuberculosis, but the doctors assured them that he would recover completely. Indeed, within a few months Mandela's health was fully restored. He had regained the lost weight and was exercising vigorously.

The government kept him at the hospital for some time. In the fall of 1988, it declared that he would not be sent back to Pollsmoor. Hope soared among Mandela's supporters. People started to believe that he and the other Rivonia prisoners would be released any day. And many of these people also believed that with Mandela's release would come sweeping changes in South Africa. To these supporters, "Mandela" meant "freedom" and "victory." Winnie told a newsmagazine, "To millions of oppressed blacks in this country and to the millions of oppressed people of all colors, Mandela's

117

name is equated with the freedom we sacrificed our lives for, for the liberation of our country.''

Yet 1988 drew to a close and Mandela was not set free. Instead, in December he was sent to Victor Verster Prison, not far from Cape Town, where he was given a comfortable house of his own, complete with television and swimming pool and allowed visits by his entire family. Although the South African government could not yet bring itself to release Mandela, it now seemed ready, even eager, to earn the world's goodwill by treating him well.

The political climate of South Africa as the 1990s approached was very different from what it had been when Mandela was imprisoned in 1962. Two and a half decades had brought many changes to the world outside the prison walls. The winds of change were blowing across South Africa.

As early as 1979, President P. W. Botha had warned the ruling Afrikaners that they would have to "adapt or die." In 1986, shortly before the United States enacted its second set of sanctions against South Africa, Botha admitted that apartheid was "outdated and unacceptable." But while many people within the South African government seemed willing to admit that change was necessary, they were very far from agreeing on just what form that change should take. And all the while, violence in South Africa—both between blacks and whites and between rival groups of blacks—was increasing. Something had to be done.

In July 1989, President Botha took the incredible action of inviting Mandela, a convicted criminal by the standards of Botha's own government, to his official mansion in Cape Town to discuss South Africa's future. Mandela accepted. The two men spent 45 minutes together, drinking tea and talking, "in a pleasant spirit," as the country's minister of justice later reported. After the meeting, Mandela announced, "I only would like to contribute to the creation of a climate which would promote peace in South Africa."

Reactions to the president's unexpected tea party were varied. Many people rejoiced, seeing it as a sign that some sort of cooperation between the government and the ANC might be possible, even after years of bitter hatred. There was also rejoicing because it now seemed obvious to all that the government was thinking about setting Mandela free. But not everyone was pleased. Some Boers who are still committed to white supremacy called President Botha a "traitor" for sitting down to talk with an admitted terrorist. And on the other side of the fence, some high-ranking members of the ANC and other anti-apartheid groups criticized Mandela for agreeing to meet with Botha without first demanding that he be set free and that the ANC and other resistance groups be unbanned.

Mandela silenced the criticism of his meeting with Botha by stating firmly from Victor Verster Prison that dialogue between the white government and the anti-apartheid movement, not armed struggle, is "the only way of ending violence and bringing peace." The following day, some black leaders who had vowed that they would never deal with the Boers except at gunpoint said that they would evaluate the idea of negotiations. The government, for its part, said that it would welcome participation from everyone who "had a commitment to peace" in the writing of a new constitution.

The way had been paved for what everyone now believed would be the next step: freedom for Nelson Mandela and perhaps the end of apartheid itself.

In September 1989, F. W. de Klerk replaced Botha as president. De Klerk was known to be more liberal, more flexible than Botha. It seemed clear that South Africa was on the verge of momentous change. A few weeks later, on October 15, Walter Sisulu and all of the other Rivonia defendants except Mandela were set free. Flags in the green, gold, and black of the ANC waved in the air over Soweto, and joyous marchers carried banners that read "Sisulu Today, Mandela Tomorrow."

It is not known why Mandela was not released at the same time as the others. Possibly because he and de Klerk had yet to agree on the terms of his release, or possibly because Mandela felt that the impact of his freedom would be greater if he were released alone after a period of suspense. But the release of Sisulu and the others suggested that the ANC would soon be allowed to function openly in South Africa after years of exile and banning. It also showed that the government was serious about moving toward some form of agreement between blacks and whites.

Sisulu and the other returning ANC leaders showed their own willingness to change by abandoning their former call for "armed struggle" and urging the Africans of the townships, especially the youth groups and gangs, to be patient and orderly and to rely on discussion, not violence. Some observers wondered whether black youngsters who had grown up on a diet of violence and utter rejection of the whites would stomach the ANC's new moderation. And everyone was still left to wonder, when would Mandela be set free?

# 11

## _The Struggle Is My Life_

EARLY IN FEBRUARY 1990, President de Klerk stood before South Africa's elected lawmakers to deliver the speech that would open a session of parliament. A few blocks away, across from Cape Town's city hall, 3,000 demonstrators had gathered to protest apartheid. One of the protest leaders was listening to de Klerk's speech over a portable radio. Suddenly she interrupted the rally with a startling announcement. De Klerk had just formally unbanned the African National Congress.

The jubilant shout of _"Amandla!"_ rose from three thousand throats, but she raised her hand for silence and shouted, with tears of joy streaming down her face, "Mandela will be free!" The crowd broke into songs, dances, and victory chants that were echoed across South Africa.

De Klerk had indeed promised to free Mandela _without conditions._ He also lifted the bans on more than 60 political organizations, including the South African Communist Party and the PAC as well as the ANC. He declared, "The season of violence is over. The time for reconciliation and reconstruction has arrived." The world held its breath, hoping that healing would truly replace killing in South Africa.

A few days later, on February 11, a peaceful crowd of hundreds of Africans waited outside the gates of the Victor Verster Prison under the watchful eyes of nervous police guards. It was a warm, sunny day, with clear skies. The watching crowd saw a string of cars crawl toward the gates from inside the prison farm. A silver sedan drove up to the gateway and then stopped. Its door swung open and a slender, gray-haired man in a dark suit stepped out. For a moment he simply gazed at the sky and the horizon as though he could hardly believe that he was standing in the open. Then he looked at the crowd that had gathered to greet him, and his gaze sharpened. He smiled broadly and raised one clenched fist, then both, in the black-power salute.

For an electric instant, Nelson Mandela and those who had gathered to greet him silently savored the sweetness of this moment. After 28 years, he was free. Many who were there had feared that this day would never come. Mandela himself had feared it. Yet at this moment all the power and hope of the African people were focused on this one slim, smiling man. Then the crowd broke into a prolonged, triumphant cheer that echoed from the prison gates and buildings. A moment later, without speaking a word, Mandela climbed back into the car for the ride into Cape Town, where he was scheduled to speak at his first public appearance since the Rivonia Trial.

The national highway leading to Cape Town was lined with throngs of supporters hoping to wave at Mandela's motorcade, so his police escort guided the motorcade along back roads to the capital city. At one stop, the three traffic policemen who accompanied the convoy on their motorcycles sent a driver to ask Mandela if he would autograph their ticket books. Smilingly, he did so. He greeted and shook hands with everyone that day, members of the Mandela Reception Committee, who accompanied him in the motorcade, the drivers of the car, people along the road, whites as well as blacks, who rushed up to take photographs of him whenever the cars stopped.

But not everything went smoothly. Authorities had been afraid that Mandela's release would spark riots, and there was some trouble from unruly groups among his supporters. Fighting broke out at several places along the highway, and the police fired into the crowd on at least one occasion. In Cape Town, more than 100,000 people had been waiting all day at a stadium called the Grand Parade to see and hear Mandela. By late afternoon, the crowd was restless. It was hot, and Mandela was overdue. Fighting and looting broke out. Angry, impatient, young people destroyed the platform that had been installed for television cameras and smashed up a car that was being used by the Reverend Jesse Jackson, who had arrived from the United States a few days earlier. Police and security guards fired into the crowd to restore order and both Jackson and the Reverend Allan Boesak urged the crowd to remain calm.

When the motorcade carrying Mandela finally arrived, his speech was delayed for nearly three more hours because both the authorities and the Mandela Reception Committee wanted to give the angry crowd time to settle down. Many people, exhausted after a day of waiting and turmoil, left the arena before he appeared.

Mandela's critics and supporters agreed that the Cape Town rally was hastily organized and badly planned. There had been too few security guards. Two days later, however, Mandela returned in triumph to Soweto, where a very successful rally was held to welcome him home. The Soweto rally was sponsored by Boesak's United Democratic Front (UDF), which was formed in 1983 as an association of trade unions, student groups, church groups, and other organizations to fight apartheid. The rally took place at the Soccer City stadium, which was crammed far past its official capacity with more than 130,000 spectators. Another 70,000 or so waited outside in the parking lot to catch a glimpse of Mandela. Volunteer marshals from the South African Youth Congress patrolled the stadium and the parking lot along with the police to keep order.

Walter Sisulu, Ahmed Kathrada, Mandela, and other ANC leaders emerged from helicopters, accompanied by their wives, and were greeted with thunderous cheers and shouts of "ANC! ANC!" and "Viva Mandela!" Sisulu made a brief introductory speech. Then came the moment that the crowd had been waiting for, for almost thirty years. Mandela stepped to the microphone and addressed the people of what was still, after all his years in prison, his hometown of Soweto.

"We are going forward," he told them. "The march toward freedom and justice is irrevers-

Afrapix, Impact Visuals

*Two days after his release from prison, Nelson Mandela returned in triumph to his hometown of Soweto. Over a hundred thousand people crammed into a soccer stadium to see him. In this photograph of the rally, Mandela greets an old friend with a warm smile.*

ible. . . . Your struggle, commitment, and your discipline have released me to stand here before you today. . . . We call upon the police to abandon apartheid and to serve the interests of the people. . . . Join our march to a new South Africa."

Then Mandela raised his fists and gave the salute that the ANC had used in the 1950s and 1960s: *"Afrika!"* Green, gold, and black balloons drifted across the hot, blue sky and drum majorettes dressed in the ANC colors twirled on the stage. Mandela returned to his helicopter and was lifted away. He went back to the Orlando house to play with his grandchildren and chat quietly with Winnie, simple pleasures that he had long been unable to enjoy.

As the weeks and months passed, the world waited to see whether Mandela would be accepted as a leader by South Africa's blacks now that he was a living, breathing man to them, leading a public life, instead of a heroic legend behind bars. The task he has taken upon himself—bringing the anti-apartheid movement and the government together to agree upon a new form of democratic, nonracial rule—is no easy one.

Centuries of hostility and mistrust between blacks and whites will not soon be overcome. Mandela has said that de Klerk and his ministers are "men of integrity" with whom he can at least open discussions, but not all whites in South Africa approve of de Klerk's moderate position. Representatives of the Conservative Party, which rejects the idea of negotiations with the ANC, stalked angrily out of parliament when President de Klerk announced that he was ready to begin discussions. And a small but outspoken group called the Afrikaner Resistance Movement, most of whose members are Boers in the Transvaal and the Orange Free State, wants whites to remain supreme in South Africa. When Mandela was released, angry members of the Afrikaner Resistance Movement marched through Pretoria with signs that read "Hang Mandela."

Some South African blacks, in turn, are unwilling to hold talks with the government and feel that they will not achieve their goals if they give up their violent resistance to the Nationalist government. The PAC, for example, favors the continuation of armed struggle—sabotage and other forms of violence—over settlement talks. A faction within the Black Consciousness group rejects the ANC's nonracial approach and insists upon black supremacy, although this position is completely rejected by Mandela and most of the influential black leaders.

Differing points of view within the African population are one reason for episodes of violence by blacks against blacks, a trend that deeply worries Mandela and other ANC leaders. This violence has roots that stretch all the way back to ancient tribal rivalries and disputes. It grew stronger during the 1980s, when militant youth groups in the black townships openly attacked Africans whom they accused of cooperating with the apartheid system, such as black police officers and rent collectors.

In recent years, fighting among black gangs and youth groups has threatened to tear apart the unity that the ANC and the UDF have built among Africans of many different backgrounds, languages, and political beliefs. In Natal Province, where the fighting has been worst, the feud between the ANC and Inkatha has caused more than 3,000 deaths since 1987. A month after his release, Mandela made an emotional plea to the warring Africans of Natal, urging them to throw their guns and knives into the sea and to work together to fight apartheid, not each other. Still, violence continues. Ending it is one of the biggest challenges that the black leadership of South Africa faces.

The Nelson Mandela of 1990 is no less committed than the Nelson Mandela of 1961 to equal rights for black South Africans, and to the end of apartheid. Those years brought South Africa to the brink of violent chaos. Nearly all of its white citizens now realize that change is inevitable. And today the majority of whites and blacks seem to think that Mandela is the spokesperson and leader who best represents the anti-apartheid point of view.

In prison, Mandela became a symbol. He was the much respected elder statesman of the anti-apartheid movement. Now, in freedom, he must survive as a practical politician if he is to see his dream of a democratic South Africa become reality. He must balance the opinions and desires of the large and often turbulent African population with the demands of the de Klerk government, without losing the confidence of either.

The first steps in this delicate balancing act took place early in May of 1990, when delegations led by Mandela and de Klerk sat down in Cape Town for talks aimed at establishing trust and outlining future discussions—what both sides called "talks about talks." For the first time since the ANC was founded, white South Africans were holding formal discussions with ANC leaders. Said Mandela, "This is the first time in 78 years that a truly serious meeting takes place between delegations of the African National Congress and the succession of white governments that have ruled our country for generations. This is a fact that is sobering in its implications."

The talks lasted for three days. The government was represented by de Klerk and several of his ministers. The ANC was represented by 11 men and women carefully chosen to represent all four of South Africa's races and a variety of political viewpoints. Mandela was clearly their leader and spokesman. At the end of the meetings, he and de Klerk appeared side by side for newspeople. Smiling at the cameras, they announced that progress had been made.

The biggest news for South Africa and the world was that the two sides had agreed on a basic goal— nothing less than the end of apartheid. They also agreed that some sort of change must be made in South Africa's form of government. Mandela and the ANC have long called for a "one person, one vote" system, which would mean that political power would be in the hands of the country's large black majority. The Nationalists, on the other hand, have declared that any change must include built-in protection for the rights and privileges of racial minorities—that is, of the whites.

The two sides are far from a compromise on this fundamental issue, but they have agreed to form committees to work on other issues, such as the release of political prisoners who remain in jail, and pardon for political exiles, such as Oliver

Tambo, who fled the country over the years to avoid persecution.

Those who expected the first meetings between the ANC and the government to bring about instant reforms were disappointed. But Mandela gently points out that such hopes are not realistic. And he is pleased that the two sides met on terms of what he describes as "cordiality." He told reporters, "We look at these discussions with satisfaction because it is a realization of a dream for which we have worked patiently and consistently over the last thirty years. Not only are we closer to one another, the ANC and the government, but we are all victors. South Africa is a victor."

The door to reconciliation has been opened. It remains to be seen whether South Africa's blacks and whites can pass through it together. Many important issues must be resolved. International economic sanctions against South Africa are still in place. Only whites have full voting rights under the current constitution. And since almost all national wealth is in the hands of white people, there is the question of economic reforms, which many blacks feel are necessary if they are to take their rightful place in their country.

Helping to resolve these issues—and to bring an end to the violence that is tearing South Africa apart—will take all the wisdom, integrity, political skill, and luck that Nelson Mandela possesses. But the man who once said, "The struggle is my life" is finally free to begin what will be his greatest struggle of all.

# PRONUNCIATION KEY
(page numbers refer to first appearance in text)

The Xhosa (Cho'-sa) language, which many black South Africans speak, uses many sounds which are not used in English. This chart will help you pronounce the Xhosa words and names you have seen in this book.

apartheid *(a-part'-hit)*, 47
Autshumayo *(Ah-tshu-moy'-yo)*, 4
Bechuanaland *(Be-kwa'-na-land)*, 83
Cofimvaba *(Co-fee-mva'-ba)*, 68
Dalibhunga *(Da-lee-bu'-nga)*, 10
Dhlomo *(Dlo'-mo)*, 44
Gaitsiwe *(Ge-tsay'-way)*, 2
Haile *(Hal)*, 85
Hlubi *(Hlu'-bee)*, 4
izinyanya *(Eezee-nya'-nya)*, 20
Jongintaba David Dalindyebo *(Jo-ngee'-nta-ba David Da-lee-ndyay'-bo)*, 14
kaross *(Ka-ross')*, 89
Khoikhoi *(Koi'-koi')*, 4
Langalibalele *(La-nga-lee-ba-lay'-lay')*, 4
mabhalane *(Ma-ba-la'-nay)*, 40
Madiba Thembikele *(Ma-dee'-ba The-mbay'-kay'-lee)*, 13
Madikizela *(Ma-dee-kee-zay'-la)*, 23
Makana *(Ma-ka'-na)*, 4
Makaziwe *(Ma-ka-zee'-way)*, 50
Makgatho *(Ma-kga'-tho)*, 50
Makholweni *(Ma-kho-lway'-nee)*, 64
Malete *(Ma-lay'-tay)*, 2
Maqoma *(Ma-ko'-ma)*, 4

132

Mapungubwe *(Ma-pu-ngu'-bway)*, 28
Mbata *(Mba'-ta)*, 36
Mbhashe *(Mba'-shay)*, 9
Mda *(M'-da)*, 55
Meintjes' Kop *(Men'-tyes Kop)*, 1
Motsamai *(Mo-tsa-mee')*, 78
Mphakanyiswa *(Mpa-ka-nyee'-swa)*, 9
Mqanduli *(Mka-ndu'-lee)*, 33
Mqekezweni *(Mkay-kay-zway'-nee)*, 15
Mqikela *(Mkee-kay'-la)*, 23
Mtirara *(Mtee-ra'-ra)*, 15
Ncome River *(Nko'-ma)*, 31
Ngangelizwe *(Nga-ngay-leez-way')*, 15
Ngubane *(Ngu-ba'-nay)*, 44
Ngubengcuka *(Ngu-bay-ngcu'-ka)*, 15
Ngutyana *(Ngu-tya'-na)*, 23
Nkosikasi *(Nko-see-ka'-zee)*, 16
Nkosi Sikelele *(Nko'-see- Si-kay-lay'-la)*, 94
Nomabandla *(No-ma-ba'-ndla)*, 13
Nomzamo Zanyiwe Winifred Madikizela *(Nom-za'-mo Za-nyee'-way Winifred Ma-dee-kee-zay'-la)*, 69
Nosekeni Fanny Mandela *(No-say-kay'-ni Fa'-ni Man-day'-la)*, 9
Ntombizodwa *(Nto-mbee-zo'-dwa)*, 16
Ntselamanzi *(Ntsay-la-ma'-nzee)*, 35
Nyerere *(Nyer-ye'-re)*, 84
Qokolweni *(Ko-ko-lway'-nee)*, 33
Qunu *(Ku'-nu)*, 10
Rolihlahla *(Ro-lee-hla'-hla)*, 10
Sobukwe *(So-bu'-kway)*, 71
Tatu Joyi *(Ta-tu Jo'-yee)*, 18
Tefu *(Tay'-fu)*, 2
Transkei *(Trans'-ki)*, 9

Tsukudu *(Tsu-ku'-du)*, 51
Umkhonto we Sizwe *(Um-ko'-nto way Si'-zway)*, 82
Vanderbijlpark *(fan-der-bal'-park)*, 72
Vereeniging *(ver-en'-e-ging)*, 72
voortrekkers *(for'-trekkers)*, 1
Xhosa *(Cho'-sa)*, 4
Zenani *(Zay-na'-nee)*, 70
Zindziswa *(Zee-ndzee'-swa)*, 70
Zwelibhangile Joyi *(Zway-lee-bha'-ngee-lay Jo'-yee)*, 18

## Other books you might enjoy reading

1. Benson, Mary. *Nelson Mandela: The Man and the Movement.* Foreword by Desmond Tutu. New York: W. W. Norton & Co., 1986.

2. Canesso, Claudia. *South Africa.* New York: Chelsea House, 1989.

3. Harrison, Nancy. *Winnie Mandela.* New York: George Braziller, Inc., 1986.

4. Haskins, Jim. *Winnie Mandela: Life of Struggle.* New York: G. P. Putnam's Sons, 1988.

5. Mandela, Nelson. *No Easy Walk To Freedom.* London: Heinemann, 1964.

6. Mandela, Nelson. *The Struggle Is My Life.* New York: Pathfinder Press, 1986.

7. Mandela, Winnie. *Part of My Soul Went with Him.* Edited by Anne Benjamin, adapted by Mary Benson. New York: W. W. Norton & Co., 1984.

8. Meer, Fatima. *Higher than Hope: The Authorized Biography of Nelson Mandela.* New York: Harper & Row, 1988.

## ABOUT THE AUTHOR

Rebecca Stefoff has written more than 40 non-fiction books for young adults, including 20 biographies, many of contemporary world leaders. She is also the author of two books on the land and people of South Africa. She lives in Philadelphia.

# THE **GREAT LIVES** SERIES...
### for
### eleven to fourteen year-old readers
### Fascinating biographies
### to
## CAPTIVATE    EDUCATE    INSPIRE
### *PICK IT UP!!!!*